Radical Intimacy

'This was my most eagerly awaited book of the last year and it does not disappoint. Sophie K. Rosa provides a clear and compelling analysis of the ways in which current social and economic conditions restrict and deny our capacity for caring relationships with ourselves and others within safe enough homes and sustainable communities, and how these conditions can be implicated in so many forms of intimate violence, injustice, loss and pain. *Radical Intimacy* is a powerful, utterly engaging read and a vital call to personal and political action. A must read.'

—Meg-John Barker, author of *Rewriting the Rules*

'In *Radical Intimacy*, Rosa proposes radical answers for people longing for real intimacy, just as she proposes the need to centre all forms of intimacy as radical praxis. We are invited to look for the possibilities of abundant postcapitalist relating right now, and how they might nurture us in overcoming the systems which trap us in scarcity. It's great. Please read it!'

—Justin Hancock, sex and relationships educator

'A clarion voice from a new generation of British feminists accessibly expanding family-abolitionist thought and praxis into new spheres in response to a swingeing care crisis. Adept at educating the reader's desire for a liveable Earth, *Radical Intimacy* is irresistible in its reasoning as to what constitutes good and bad ways of organising dying, pair-bonding, therapy, kinship, urban habitation, people-making, and so much more besides. In this beautiful and well-researched meditation on intimate comradeliness, Rosa lays out what it will take to make "impossible families possible" and, in the meantime, proliferate "friendship in and against the state". A book that will convince many on the left to centre the rubric of care at last, even though capitalism is (of course) doing its best to co-opt it. I was gripped.'

—Sophie Lewis, author of *Abolish the Family*

'Sophie K. Rosa's call for "radical intimacies" highlights the cruelty and scarcity of care in capitalist and colonial forms of relating. Readers who feel the terrible pain of ruling-class intimacy, but who have not yet encountered more collectivist support, love and attention, will be especially grateful for Rosa's words. This book that explores Black and Indigenous feminist and queer revolutionary approaches to relating helps unshackle the mind from capitalist and colonial kinship, friendship and romance. In order to change the world, one must first change the story of the world that is possible. *Radical Intimacy* helps us do that.'

—Professor Kim TallBear, University of Alberta

'Made me reconsider so many of the cultural scripts I've been fed my whole life. Unsparing, important and hopeful.'

—Annie Lord, author of *Notes on Heartbreak*

Radical Intimacy

Sophie K. Rosa

PLUTO PRESS

First published 2023 by Pluto Press
New Wing, Somerset House, Strand, London WC2R 1LA
and Pluto Press Inc.
1930 Village Center Circle, 3-834, Las Vegas, NV 89134

www.plutobooks.com

British Library Cataloguing in Publication Data
A catalogue record for this book is available from the British Library

ISBN   978 0 7453 4516 1   Paperback
ISBN   978 0 7453 4521 5   PDF
ISBN   978 0 7453 4520 8   EPUB

This book is printed on paper suitable for recycling and made from fully
managed and sustained forest sources. Logging, pulping and manufacturing
processes are expected to conform to the environmental standards of the
country of origin.

Typeset by Stanford DTP Services, Northampton, England

Simultaneously printed in the United Kingdom and United States of America

Contents

Introduction: the intimate is political

People who talk about revolution and class struggle without referring explicitly to everyday life, without understanding what is subversive about love and what is positive in the refusal of constraints, such people have a corpse in their mouth.

Raoul Vaneigem

Certain modes of relating can crack us open ...
We think this practice is ultimately connected to
what will allow us to stop going to work, to take what we
    need.
We are learning how to unleash our desires to the point
    that they rupture with capital.
    Clémence x. Clémentine/infinite venom association

Writing this book during the Covid-19 pandemic, its themes felt raw, sometimes too raw to touch. The meaning of 'intimacy' shifted as 'social distancing' became the norm; the relationship between 'closeness' and 'care' changed overnight. All at once, we were confronted with ourselves, with each other and with the state of everything around us. As the scope of our days contracted, our emotional lives and relationships were magnified. To start with, there was much talk of the crisis being an opportunity to take stock, to decipher what really matters and rebuild from there. As the government failed to take effective action to save lives and the death toll began to rise, anxiety, fear and chaos took hold. It became

1

clearer than ever that we need each other in order to be well, to survive. But in many cases we lacked the language, modes and infrastructure to express – much less meet – that need. Many people found themselves stranded.

'Intimacy' is primal and inscrutable, vital and elusive. Like love, it is difficult to explain for good reason: something so intricately personal – spiritual – might be debased by attempts at objective definition. Nevertheless, I will attempt to discern what 'intimacy' might mean, and to explain how I understand it for the purposes of this book.

Upon learning 'intimacy' was its subject, some people assumed this book would be about sex. Indeed, 'to be intimate' is often used euphemistically in this way. Intimacy is much more (and much less) than sex – though perhaps sex itself could be a helpful lens through which to understand it. Whilst intimacy in general need not include any semblance of sex, as an experience it might mirror some of the reasons people can find sex meaningful. Like sex, intimacy can allow us to access desire, pleasure, comfort, tending, tenderness, coming together and feelings of 'being seen'. But just as not all sex is intimate, not all intimacy is sexual. 'Intimacy' encompasses many kinds of relationships. It is a way of being together that might include fleeting or enduring experiences of affinity, vulnerability, nearness and love.

The intimate realm has broader valence, too. It can refer to the textures of the personal and the everyday; the essence of our lives. Moreover, it can be, as the geographer Paul Jackson suggests, 'a form of commoning' that 'is often arduous'. It is, as he writes, 'overdetermined by desire, but can also be built upon common suffering'.[1]

My use of 'intimate' draws upon all these understandings to compose a rubric that includes connection, care and community; put another way: relationships, social reproduction and kinship. In this book, I consider intimacy via different topics: self-care, romantic love and sex, family, home, death and friendship.

Initially, I imagined this book being called *Intimate Comrades*, as I wanted the title to capture the co-constitution of intimacy and struggles for a better world. My editor was not sold on 'comrades', however – if only because it might be off-putting for some prospective readers not, shall we say, 'on the left'. He proposed *Radical Intimacy* instead, and I had initial reservations. I was concerned that people might interpret the term as prescriptive, and assume my book would advocate for specific, 'radical' forms of intimacy. It is certainly not my intention to do so.

What, then, might 'radical intimacy' mean? At first sight, the term could be interpreted as an 'extreme' intimacy: deep intimacy as symbiosis. This is not really what 'radical intimacy' refers to here; though it is not *not* this, either. Rather, 'radical' is used to refer to political radicalism: a politics with imagination and abolitionism at its core, that seeks to transform the world by *getting to the root* of why things are the way they are under capitalism. For example, rather than campaigning for more police on the streets to 'protect women', a radical feminist politics demands police abolition, identifying the carceral state as a root of patriarchal violence.* Or, as opposed to more lenient border enforcement to make life better for migrants, a radical demand would be border abolition, rec-

---

* It is well evidenced that police and prisons not only fail to keep women safe from gendered violence but endanger them further. For example, in 2020 in England and Wales, just 1.6% of reported rape cases resulted in a charge or summons. In 2019, the Centre for Women's Justice put forward a super-complaint to the prison inspectorate claiming a 'systemic failure' to safeguard women abused by police officers and staff. A 1990s report found that at least 40 per cent of police officers in the United States were violent towards their partners, in contrast to 10 per cent of the general public.

3

ognising that borders are not immutable and that their very existence is a root of racist violence. Abolition insists upon nothing less than liberation; as the prison abolitionist and scholar Ruth Wilson Gilmore has said, it 'is about presence, not absence. It's about building life-affirming institutions.'[2]

In this way, 'radical intimacy' aims to *get to the root* of intimacy as we know it. It explores the ways capitalism psychically and materially predetermines, infiltrates and thwarts our intimate lives. It reflects upon why this matters, and what resistance in this realm could mean. Radical intimacy considers, as the scholar and filmmaker Susan Stryker writes, how the state and its ideologies often 'regulate bodies, in ways both great and small, by enmeshing them within norms and expectations that determine what kinds of lives are deemed livable or useful and by shutting down the space of possibility and imaginative transformation where peoples' lives begin to exceed and escape the state's use for them'.[3] Radical intimacy insists that to remake the world we must pay attention to connection, care and community as sites of struggle. Doing so could bring us closer – to ourselves and to each other – in ways that fuel our struggles towards revolutionary horizons.

'Capitalism' is a socio-economic system in which life is organised such that profit is prioritised over everything else. This system rests upon the private ownership of the means of production* (by the bourgeoise) and the exploitation of labour power (of the proletariat). The origins of capitalism are contested, but regardless of which account you turn to the capitalist mode of production has been around for no more than a few hundred years, growing in northwest Europe before spreading across the planet, including via colonialism. Capitalism has many stages and varieties, though today the word is

---

* The elements required to produce goods and services: labour, land and capital.

4

often used as a catch-all for our profit-driven society and what it feels like to live in it. In this book, I use 'capitalism' to refer to this socio-economic system, as well as the attendant forms of oppression it depends upon, including racism and sexism. Sometimes I refer to specific oppressive systems, other times I use 'capitalism' as shorthand for the system that the scholar and activist bell hooks describes as 'imperialist white-supremacist capitalist patriarchy'.

The personal is political

A theoretical foundation for this book is that 'the personal is political'. Popular in the 1970s second-wave feminist movement, the slogan was coined in response to increasing criticism from leftist men that women's liberation, unlike class struggle, was not 'real' or 'serious' politics. Women's oppression under capitalism – including issues such as sexual violence, access to abortion and the distribution of domestic and caring labour – was frequently dismissed by male-dominated radical movements as a personal problem, as opposed to the basis for feminist solidarity. The political work of 'conscious-ness-raising' groups, in which women gathered to discuss and find collective solutions for what the feminist scholar Helen Hester has called 'the material hegemonies of gendered life', was belittled.[4] 'The personal is political' insists that the details of our lives can reveal structural power and oppression. As Michèle Barrett and Mary McIntosh argued in their 1982 work *The Anti-social Family*, a key tenet of 'the personal is political' is 'the idea of public discussion about personal life' as an important component of radical politics.[5] This book aims to contribute to ongoing discussions of that ilk.

The 1970s feminist movement was part of a contemporane-ous global mass revolt confronting the systemic oppressions of capitalism, including state violence and racism. Radical

feminists and queers of this era often opposed the patriarchal nuclear family as the primary site of women's oppression
and exploitation for the reproduction of the capitalist system.
Many experimented with unconventional relationships and
ways of organising care. The Third World Women's Alliance
– a US political group formed in 1968 to centre women of
colour's struggles in revolutionary feminism – described its
position on the nuclear family thus:

> Whereas in a capitalist culture, the institution of the family
> has been used as an economic and psychological tool, not
> serving the needs of people, we declare that we will not
> relate to the private ownership of any person by another. We
> encourage and support the continued growth of communal
> households and the idea of the extended family. We encour-
> age alternative forms to the patriarchal family and call for
> the sharing of all work (including housework and child
> care) by men and women.[6]

By the 1980s, radical political movements faced widespread
defeat. Feminism broadly settled on a reformist approach: an
equality and rights-based platform that did not pose a significant threat to capitalism. Feminism in the UK today reflects
this. The mainstream movement privileges white, bourgeois
and corporate interests, and has become associated with pro-
carceral, trans-exclusionary and anti-sex work positions that
are incompatible with feminism's central purposes of liberation from gender roles, gendered oppression and violence, and
bodily and sexual autonomy for all.

There is, however, a radical counter-current in feminism
in the UK and elsewhere today, which is reviving critiques
of the nuclear family, social reproduction and sexual politics,
and foregrounding anti-racism and abolitionism. My writing
here owes much to this resurgent anti-capitalist feminism and

is inspired by the foundational work of Black and Indigenous feminisms, and queer and utopian revolutionary thinking.

The case for radical intimacy

Foregrounding connection, care and community in our political analyses and action can be powerful. Our intimate lives are the source of our heaviest sufferings and most relieving joys, and present ardent opportunities for transformation. Our intimate experiences, feelings and longings give our lives meaning. They can give us reasons to stay alive. The reality, though, is that intimacy in the world as we know it is often lacking. As the cultural theorist Lauren Berlant has said: 'It's a heartbreak that the world isn't worth ... our attachment to it, that it gives us objects or ways of life or forms of life that are constantly betraying us.'[7] Our normative modes of relating and living often fall short – both in meeting our intimate needs and in allowing us to form and build the kinds of relationships that could support our struggles for a future of abundance, rather than recreate the privation of the status quo.

The intimate realm is devalued on the left today, both in mainstream and radical ambits. This neglect not only overlooks the terrain's latent power for political movements, but sidelines many liberation struggles. For example, traditional labour organising mostly ignores social reproduction such as care work – paid or unpaid – which is largely done by women, especially racialised and migrant women, often in private homes. Ignoring or diminishing the importance of the intimate realm, too, devalues the experiences of trans and queer people, for whom normative intimate forms, such as heteronormative relationships and the nuclear family, are often exclusionary and oppressive. Revaluing intimacy, then, becomes a strategy to resist heteropatriarchy, which underpins capitalism, and therefore to strengthen our revolutionary movements.

A political commitment to the intimate realm also counterposes capitalism's dictate that existence is about work and not much more. Indeed, whilst worker organising is at the core of anti-capitalism, a reduction of our politics to labour struggles *and little else* not only implies a resignation to 'life as work' but disregards the fact that many people cannot or do not labour for a wage. As the activist Steve Graby writes in relation to the disabled people's movement, 'a vital component in the struggle against capitalism is "self-valorization", or the autonomous construction of ethical values counter to those of a society based on authority and exploitation, in order to not merely react reflexively to specific attacks by capital, but to positively and creatively re-invent social relations'.[8]

Paying attention to intimacy is crucial when building political movements. The intimate sphere is central to our emotional lives, and thus a potent site ripe for transformation. In this vein, considering the ways capitalism infuses our loving relationships, the sociologist and political economist Emma Dowling argues: 'As our material precarity increases, rejecting precariousness in our love relations would be a good place to start to build affective resistance and with that, other possible worlds of love and care.'[9] Our intimate lives are the crux of reproducing – or not – life itself. Our relationships and kinship forms remake the world and, as such, are critical to our struggles for a better one. As feminist activists and scholars Camille Barbagallo and Silvia Federici put it: 'the struggle over "reproduction" is central to every other struggle and to the development of "self-reproducing movements", that is movements that do not separate political work from the activities necessary to the reproduction of our life, for no struggle is sustainable that ignores the needs, experiences, and practices that reproducing ourselves entails'.[10]

Intimacy is essential as well as the terrain of pleasure and peak experience. Normative modes of intimacy often limit its potential, while our experiences and material conditions can make it hard to imagine, let alone desire, our lives being any other way. Imagining that things could be radically different can be a way to reject the exploitation, oppression and violence in the world, helping us reimagine ourselves as capable of rebellion. This relates to what the writer and activist adrienne maree brown calls 'pleasure activism': 'the work we do to reclaim our whole, happy, and satisfiable selves from the impacts, delusions, and limitations of oppression and/or supremacy'. According to brown, pleasure activism insists that 'we all need and deserve pleasure and that our social structures must reflect this', and that 'we must prioritize the pleasure of those most impacted by oppression'.[11] As the author Kay Gabriel writes in relation to trans liberation, 'the desire for a disalienated life-world – as envisioned in the slogan bread and roses – is if nothing else the demand for everyone to enjoy the kinds of aesthetic contingency that capital cordons off for the wealthy. As a result any genuine revolutionary politics will orient itself towards a radically pleasurable future.'[12]

An overview of this book (and some considerations)

This book explores intimacy in the context of capitalism through a series of topics: self-care, romantic love and sex, the family, home, death and friendship. These themes are intended as helpful lenses, rather than purporting to cover every aspect or possible framing of the intimate realm. Each chapter looks at how a particular arena of intimacy exists in relation to capitalism, considers how this might be impacting, limiting or harming us, then explores how things could be otherwise. Moreover, each chapter considers the ways in which

the intimate realm can impede or facilitate political transformation, asking what it could mean to position intimacy as a
site of struggle in our movements for a future with more connection, more care and more community/communality. In
every case, the book aims to be attentive to the fact that, in
society as it stands, there is no way of doing intimacy that will,
on its own, transform our lives, let alone the world – or, as the
feminist organiser Carol Hanisch put it in 1969, that 'all alternatives are bad under present conditions'.[13] To be manageable
in scope, the book focuses on the context of the UK, though
examples from other places are sometimes included.

Considering the decisive ways that capitalism config-
ures existence, it is an important framework through which
to understand life – but it is not the only one. Our desires,
emotions and decisions have many origins. Whilst the
economic system might helpfully be considered the umbrella
under which all else is formed, it is also true that our lives are
subject to other, sometimes more mysterious, forces. Psy-
choanalytic theory, for instance, considers the powerful sway
that the unconscious mind has over our lives – for example
by compelling us to repeat certain behaviours stemming from
past experiences.

Waking up and remaking the world

Paraphrasing the philosopher John Holloway, David Graeber
writes that capitalism 'only exists because every day we wake
up and continue to produce it. If we woke up one morning
and all collectively decided to produce something else, then
we wouldn't have capitalism anymore.'[14] It is a tragedy that
most of us, surely, would not choose to live in a world like
this. We did not consent to the conditions of our lives, and yet
we feel powerless to change them. The 'ultimate revolution-

ary question', then, writes Graeber, is 'what are the conditions that would have to exist to enable us to do this – to just wake up and imagine and produce something else?' As we contend apocalyptic times, I hope this book contributes to the task of answering this question.

CHAPTER ONE

Your life in your hands

I am often struck by the dangerous narcissism fostered by
spiritual rhetoric that pays so much attention to individual
self-improvement and so little to the practice of love within
the context of community.

bell hooks

We gotta keep each other alive any way we can 'cause
nobody else is goin' do it.

Larry Mitchell

In November 2021, the therapy app BetterHelp partnered with
rapper and record producer Travis Scott after ten people died
and hundreds were injured in a crowd surge at his Astroworld
Festival in Houston, Texas. Prior to the 50,000-people event,
local authorities had expressed safety concerns,[1] and following the disaster, Scott and the organisers faced numerous
lawsuits claiming negligence and incitement. In response to
the tragedy, Scott offered gig attendees one month of free
therapy on BetterHelp. Controversy ensued, as BetterHelp
and Scott were accused of profiting off people's suffering.
Though Scott denied being paid for the brand partnership
(Astroworld grossed $53.5 million in 2019 – he could afford
not to), the offer was nonetheless part of a marketing strategy.

Scott's press release after the Astroworld disaster read:
'Travis is grateful to be working alongside BetterHelp, a
renowned mental health service provider.' However, Better-
Help – the Uber of mental health services – is notorious.

The app's own website has a footnote regarding its therapeutic limitations: 'If you are in a crisis or any other person may be in danger – don't use this site', reads the ambiguous disclaimer.

In exchange for a monthly charge of around £200 to £300 per month, BetterHelp enables people seeking mental health support to communicate with a therapist in a 24/7 'room' using video calls, phone calls, live chats and text messages. In reviews of BetterHelp, people share stories alleging unhelpful or harmful therapy, data privacy concerns, excessive charges, and having their sessions suddenly terminated. If it is difficult to regulate in-person therapy, it is even harder on an app. BetterHelp's Terms of Service reads (in capital letters):

YOU HEREBY RELEASE US AND AGREE TO HOLD US HARMLESS FROM ANY AND ALL CAUSES OF ACTION AND CLAIMS OF ANY NATURE RESULTING FROM THE THERAPIST SERVICES OR THE PLATFORM, INCLUDING (WITHOUT LIMITATION) ANY ACT, OMISSION, OPINION, RESPONSE, ADVICE, SUGGESTION, INFORMATION AND/OR SERVICE OF ANY THERAPIST...

Raising complaints with BetterHelp might prove difficult; 'help' is mostly algorithmically managed. For therapists, BetterHelp is gig economy work: unpredictable and highly demanding, with much lower rates of pay than other avenues of employment.[2]

BetterHelp's partnership with Travis Scott is part of the platform's established advertising strategy, often involving marketing deals with Instagram influencers and celebrities. In 2018, scandal hit the app after well-known YouTubers began creating BetterHelp-sponsored content, baring their souls on camera before urging viewers to sign up to the therapy platform, earning them commission via affiliate links. A backlash accused such sponsorship deals of being unethical and BetterHelp of being a 'scam'.[3]

As the lethal chaos unfolded at Astroworld, young fans shared horrifying videos on TikTok of people – moments before in 'post-pandemic' ecstasy – being crushed in the crowd, their guttural pleas for help drowned out by the music. In *Ghosts of My Life: Writings on Depression, Hauntology and Lost Futures*, the cultural critic and theorist Mark Fisher posits that hip-hop might be where 'the secret sadness lurk[ing] behind the 21st century's forced smile' has 'registered most deeply'. Popular artists such as Kanye West and Drake, who performed with Scott at Astroworld, he suggests, are 'morbidly fixated on exploring the miserable hollowness at the core of super-affluent hedonism'.[4]

What Fisher calls the 'hedonist's sadness' of the conspicuous consumer drenches the Astroworld footage. In one YouTube clip – entitled 'The moment Travis Scott knew there was something wrong in the audience', viewed almost a million times – the star, having paused the show, appears to briefly leave his body, gazing in terror at the desperate situation. Moments later he screams for everyone 'to make this motherfucking ground shake'. Once again, urgent cries are rendered futile as Scott begins to perform the eerie 'Lost Forever', which includes lyrics promoting Dior. 'It's hard not to hear', writes Fisher, 'demands that we enjoy ourselves as thin attempts to distract from a depression that they can only mask, never dissipate'.[5]

How are we doing?

The collision of obligatory peak enjoyment with profound suffering is characteristic of social forces that compel success and happiness whilst materially producing impoverished lives

– whether economically, socially or spiritually. Meaningful statistics on rates of mental illness over time are hard to come by because of changing understandings and diagnoses, as well as the inconsistency with which people self-report symptoms in surveys. However, many studies show that depression and anxiety rates have increased greatly over the past few decades, especially since the 1980s.[6] In 2019, the suicide rate for men hit a two-decade high.[7]

The Covid-19 pandemic has brought mental health to the fore. According to data from the Office for National Statistics, one in five people now experience moderate to severe symptoms of depression – with women, young people, poor people and disabled people most impacted – compared to one in ten before the pandemic.[8] Another study by Mind shows that existing inequalities in housing, employment, finances and other areas made the mental health impact of the pandemic worse for racialised groups.[9] Ten million people, including 1.5 million children, will likely require new or additional mental health support as a direct result of the crisis, according to the Royal College of Psychiatrists (RCP). Meanwhile, RCP president Adrian James described the pandemic as likely being 'the biggest hit to mental health since the second world war'.[10] Even before these statistics were available, government communications as well as corporate advertising – harnessing a general sense that a global pandemic, mass death, widespread fear, increased hardship, domestic isolation and repeated lockdowns were likely to do *something* to people's psychological well-being – told us to 'check-in on each other' and 'stay connected'. To the state this meant, 'keep calm and carry on as we kill you'; to advertisers it meant, 'buy this to make your isolation, dread and sickness more bearable'.

Under capitalism, mental health is understood as a personal failing, rather than the result of societal forces. Someone who is depressed, for example, is likely to find their depression is theorised by institutions and authorities – such as the medical profession, bosses, the Department for Work and Pensions, and often their family – as an individualised problem. Depression may be understood as a lack of 'get up and go', an inability to 'get over' difficult experiences, or perhaps as only a chemical imbalance that can be remedied by the person's own efforts or medication alone. Acknowledging the *social* causes of mental illness or distress, by contrast, allows us to consider how the world is making us unwell. In turn, this may alleviate suffering and energise resistance because, as Fisher writes:

> Depression is partly constituted by a sneering 'inner' voice which accuses you of self-indulgence – you aren't depressed, you're just feeling sorry for yourself, pull yourself together ... Of course, this voice isn't an 'inner' voice at all – it is the internalised expression of actual social forces, some of which have a vested interest in denying any connection between depression and politics.[11]

When David Cameron became prime minister in 2010 – placing the country in Tory hands from which it has yet to escape – his government implemented austerity measures in welfare, healthcare and education that would intensify the stress and struggle of people's lives in the aftermath of the longest and deepest recession in a generation. Papering over the material and psychological impact of such measures, Cameron also vowed to increase the nation's well-being with a 'happiness agenda'. Thus the government claimed to care about people's well-being whilst simultaneously inflicting mental torture via neoliberal economic policies.

According to recent research, procedures for out-of-work benefit claims became more 'institutionally violent' between 2010 and 2015, with 'psychological harm [used] as a technique' to deter claimants and avoid paying them. Carrying out in-depth interviews with frontline workers and managers in public and contracted employment services, the researchers uncovered 'an array of policy tools and hidden managerial methods used during the coalition administration, [which] encouraged frontline staff to deliver services in ways that led to a range of harmful outcomes for benefit claimants' in the attempt to coerce them into work.[12] People claiming benefits during this time reported mental illness being precipitated or exacerbated by such a regime,[13] and nothing has improved since. The benefits system overall is still shaped by reforms introduced from 2010. Indeed, since welfare tends to become more punitive in periods following a major crisis, such as a pandemic-induced recession, the system of state 'support' will continue inflicting – likely increasing – harm.

Margaret Thatcher once stated that 'Economics are the method; the object is to change the heart and soul.' Since human 'hearts and souls' cannot be subsumed into the logic of capital without alienation and varying types and degrees of immiseration, the changes Thatcher refers to could in part be understood as mental illness. In this vein, the 1970s revolutionary therapy collective 'Red Therapy' described mental illness as 'a major form of reaction, of our bodies' rebellion, against capitalism'.[14]

The need to sell our labour power for a wage in order to survive causes suffering. Whether we are unemployed, underemployed, in in-work poverty, enduring poor working conditions, underpaid, unpaid or overworked – or in a combination of these states – work as we know it is our poisonous lifeblood. Most people spend a large proportion of their waking hours working, and much of their 'free time' exhausted by work. According to some analyses, the pandemic has woken many up to this tragedy: people are quitting their jobs in record numbers in what has been dubbed 'the Great Resignation'.[15]

Sadly, for most of us, there is no escaping labour, and the future of work looks bleak. The 2010s were the worst decade for real wage growth since the Napoleonic wars, and stagnation is projected to continue. Work is increasingly precarious and insecure, with people facing intense competition for jobs they don't want and anxiety about automation rendering their skills obsolete. The gig economy – in which workers are even more disposable, harder to unionise, and have fewer rights and protections – is booming, while the boundaries between work and home, and work and 'free time', are becoming increasingly blurry.

The pressure to self-commodify is intense, whether by accruing 'positive reviews' on the apps we depend upon for work, or by constructing 'strong personal branding' on social media. This phenomenon is captured by psychoanalyst and philosopher Erich Fromm's concept of 'the marketing character' – 'experiencing oneself as a commodity, and one's value not as "use value" but as "exchange value"'[16] – which serves as a source of alienation, spiritual depletion and suffering. The idea of human life as capital needing to accrue value is instilled from childhood, especially so in millennials, argues Malcolm Harris in *Kids These Days*, with anxiety and depression among young people consequently significantly higher than in previous generations.[17]

The increasing 'flexibilisation' of work might be considered capitalism's appropriation of growing anti-work sentiment. 'I choose to WORK around my social life', reads a London Underground poster advert for 'gig: The Flexible Working App'. 'Damilola' has '140 Gigs', claims the advert – including 'COVID-19 Tester', 'Warehouse Operative' and 'Customer Care Steward'. This façade of freedom is anything but.

In neoliberalism, suggests the political theorist Franco Berardi in *Precarious Rhapsody*, 'The person is free, sure. But his time is enslaved. His liberty is a juridical fiction to which nothing in concrete daily life corresponds.'[18] At work, people are increasingly subject to anxiety-inducing surveillance via technologies that quantify their productivity, and sometimes purportedly their health and well-being. Amazon has become the malignant poster child for the widespread reality of soul-crushing micro-management, with its targets that leave delivery workers no time to use the toilet, or its patented wristbands designed to maximise warehouse productivity by tracking workers' every move, using 'haptic feedback' vibrations to steer their bodies.[19] The combination of precarity with intensifying self-quantification and digital connectivity creates 'constant attentive stress', writes Berardi, and 'a reduced time available for affectivity', which 'provoke[s] an effect of devastation on the individual psyche: depression, panic, anxiety, the sense of solitude and existential misery'. This is not a personal inability to cope, he emphasises, but 'a growing mass of existential misery that is tending always more to explode in the center of the social system'.[20]

In lives dominated by work, in treadmill-like cities – full of people, yet defined by segregation and isolation – people often experience feelings of alienation. The dominant architecture is designed to protect and facilitate profit. Office blocks replace social housing; gated developments are marketed to individuals, couples and nuclear families; 'designing out crime' police officers influence the built environment to minimise social interaction.[21] A sense of security among loving community is hard to come by, and solidarity with our neighbours perhaps even harder. Beyond casual greetings – or the odd 'excuse me' or 'sorry' or 'thank you' or 'fuck you' – speaking to each other, let alone caring for each other, outside of private homes, transactions, workplaces or planned socialising, is uncommon, even considered suspect.

We live with the knowledge that the economic system in which we exist is wreaking havoc on our planet. The most recent global climate summit failed to produce an agreement that will limit temperature increases to below 2°C, a rise that will devastate life on Earth, with people living in the Global South and low-income marginalised groups facing much higher threats to their health and survival.

Ecological crisis is linked to somatic and psychic crisis. Air pollution, for example, damages our bodies systemically – harming every organ, almost every cell, and our mental health.[22] A recent study found a clear relationship between rising temperatures and suicide rates, and clear evidence for the climate crisis exacerbating mental distress.[23] The researchers also found that mentally ill people are more vulnerable to the health effects of climate change, and that the climate crisis threatens to disrupt existing mental health care. The depletion of the planet correlates with the depletion of ourselves, writes literary critic Mikkel Krause Frantzen: 'The perpetuum mobile of capitalism and its exhaustion of resources also pertains to mental resources. The economic and the psychological seem to have become indistinguishable from each other, as the double meaning of depression would also suggest.'[24]

Meanwhile, dominant culture preaches happiness – with ourselves and with the world – as aspirational, selling us avenues to wellness. In *The Happiness Industry*, William Davies argues that the elusive feeling of 'happiness' is increasingly monitored and manipulated – through surveillance technologies, algorithmic advertising and psychological profiling – by state and corporate bodies, to produce docile and efficient subjects.[25] This kind of happiness is vacuous, proclaiming – as self-described 'Black, lesbian, mother, warrior, poet' Audre Lorde put it in *The Cancer Journals* – 'Let us seek "joy" rather than real food and clean air and a saner future on a liveable earth! As if happiness alone can protect us from the results of profit-madness.'[26]

The 'joy' we are supposed to seek is associated with some life paths and not others. As Sara Ahmed writes in *The Promise of Happiness*, theorists have long shown 'how happiness is used to justify oppression' and to 'redescribe social norms as social goods', in 'Feminist critiques of the figure of "the happy housewife", black critiques of the myth of "the happy slave", and queer critiques of the sentimentalization of heterosexuality as "domestic bliss".'[27]

Fighting to overthrow the system could feel like a salve for the suffering of life under capitalism. But revolutionary work can also leave us depleted. It might even feel impossible or futile. Dissent is increasingly prevented and punished by the state with tactics such as surveillance, stop-and-search, police raids, mass arrests and tighter border controls. Passed in April 2022, the Police, Crime, Sentencing and Courts Act is now stifling resistance further, having increased police powers and created new offences criminalising protest.

'Political depression', writes Ann Cvetkovich in *Depression: A Public Feeling*, is 'the sense that customary forms of political response, including direct action and critical analysis, are no longer working either to change the world or to make us feel better'.[28] For some people, this affective state might entail despair or inertia; for others, it might lead them to reactionary politics. Fisher considered the rise of the far right, including the social mood resulting in Brexit and the rise of Trump, as a counterforce to increasing resignation about depressing living conditions – a last-ditch attempt at upending them, at whatever cost. 'There is a connection between capitalist realism and depressive realism', writes Fisher. 'The idea that life is essentially drudgery (and that therefore no one should get a free ride) is a depressive conception of fairness (if I have to be miserable, so should everyone else), which has a particular traction in a burnt-out post-protestant culture like

England's ... (England is the oldest capitalist country, don't forget...).'[29]

Are you getting help?

Comprehending suffering as a collective experience, and locating its origins in the system around us, may help us to understand ourselves and each other, and to lessen the burden of mainstream, individualising discourses on mental health. But, as Cvetkovich writes: 'Saying that capitalism (or colonialism or racism) is the problem does not help me get up in the morning.'[30] Whilst some stridently believe that mental illness is a personal problem, and others just as ardently that it is 'capitalism's fault', it can also be understood as biopsychosocial: caused by an interconnection of biological factors such as hormones, psychological factors such as trauma history, and social factors such as racism.

Whatever the reasons we suffer, our options for support usually range from woefully inadequate to actively harmful. A decade of austerity has wrought havoc on people's wellbeing at the same time as decimating NHS mental health services, which face a severe lack of funding and resources. Disappearing community services, staff shortages and growing waiting lists mean that it can be near-impossible to access vital support. As recently revealed by the *Guardian*, the NHS is paying £2bn a year to private hospitals to receive mental health patients because of bed shortages – despite concerns that these institutions are routinely unsafe.[31]

Aside from the scarce free or low-cost options made available by some private practices, appropriate and effective therapeutic options are mostly reserved for those with the money, time and resources to access them. And even then, being in therapy isn't necessarily therapeutic. As members of society, therapists can and do reinforce hateful ideologies such as racism, transphobia and whorephobia (demonstrating they're not 'apolitical', as they might claim, at all).

For those unable to access private therapists, NHS talking therapy is available through Improving Access to Psychological Therapies (IAPT) services, launched by Tony Blair's 'happiness tsar' Lord Richard Layard in 2008. Replacing many other forms of counselling and psychotherapy offered by GP surgeries and the third sector, most of the free therapy provision in the UK is now short-term cognitive behavioural therapy (CBT), often outsourced to private companies. CBT adopts a medicalised, 'evidence-based' approach to mental illness, aiming to treat 'negative' thought patterns – as symptoms of diagnoses such as 'social phobia' or 'panic disorder' – as quickly as possible. Whilst helpful for some people, the use of CBT can be motivated by getting people off benefits and 'back to work', rather than exploring the roots of suffering in personal histories and social contexts. CBT as a 'one-size-fits-all' approach fails many. Of those deemed 'suitable for treatment' with IAPT – those with symptoms that aren't judged to be too severe, complex or persistent – around half receive one-to-one talking therapy. Increasingly, 'low-intensity' therapies are offered, online or via apps. And even though, according to many measures, Black people – with experiences of intergenerational trauma and racism – experience higher levels of mental distress, they are less likely to receive NHS therapy.

The apparent success of IAPT is quantified in 'performance data' that includes a 'recovery rate' measured in terms of 'caseness', i.e. whether the patient is considered a 'clinical case' at the end of their treatment, as measured by algorithmic scores derived from diagnostic questionnaires. Questions on the generalised anxiety disorder 'scale' ask people how often (0, not at all; to 3, nearly every day) they have been, for example, 'worrying too much about different things', or 'feeling afraid as if something awful might happen'. Being 'recovered' means scoring lower on these diagnostic question-naires after a period of therapy.

Whilst acknowledging that IAPT services help some people simply by providing a space for their feelings to be heard, the psychotherapist Paul Atkinson, who helps to run the Free Psychotherapy Network, considers the quantifi-cations of 'recovery' in CBT 'assembly-line fixes for the madness of living under neoliberalism'.[32] Symptoms that this kind of therapy might consider 'mental illness' could, rather, be seen as sane responses to being alive in the world. What is 'worrying too much about different things' if we are struggling to pay our rent and feed our children, or facing transpho-bia that makes being in public space frightening? How do we maintain an awareness of the gravity of the ecological crisis, and so organise for climate justice, without 'feeling afraid as if something awful might happen'? How can the ability to work be considered recovery, if it is work that is making us sick?

Despite the state of the world, we are pushed, even coerced, towards wellness. The 'self-care' industry markets solutions to suffering based on a pro-capitalist conception of wellness. 'Good self-care' might include signing up to yoga and med-itation apps, using skincare products and sex toys, ingesting expensive and foul substances like 'functional mushroom tea', or watching Netflix. But these activities are only considered healthy if they bolster rather than subtract from the time and/or energy we dedicate to work. This understanding of self-care is attached to productivity, or, as feminist activists and scholars Silvia Federici and Nicole Cox put it, to 'preparing ourselves for work ... restoring our "muscles, nerves, bones and brains" with quick snacks, quick sex, movies...'.[33]

Included in 'self-care' might be various forms of 'self-help'. On some meditation and mindfulness apps, users offer up personal data, often shared with third parties for advertising or marketing purposes, in exchange for free mental health support. Such apps are sometimes 'prescribed' by employers to serve as mental health support for workers, in lieu of improving the pay or working conditions that may be causing their distress in the first place. 'Happier people. Healthier business' promises the mindfulness app Headspace, on its page advertising the platform as 'the only employee mental health solution for modern organizations that combines a popular, science-based application with a program fit for the enterprise'. Like the growing popularity of psychedelics in Silicon Valley, self-administered app therapy may in the end amount to a kind of self-development more helpful to profit growth than to emotional growth. No matter how we are feeling, 'sanity' under capitalism is about the willingness and ability to work – the harder, the better.

Therapy and self-care might alleviate suffering. They might also be understood as forms of adaptation to, or even collusion with, its underlying causes. 'The well-balanced person', wrote the philosopher Theodor W. Adorno, 'would not thereby have achieved an inner resolution of social conflicts' because 'His integration would be a false reconciliation with an unreconciled world.' At worst, he conjectured, this kind of 'false reconciliation' could be 'an "identification with the aggressor", a mere character-mask of subordination' to systems of violence, stifling solidarity and dissent.[34]

Staying, or *seeming* to have stayed, 'sane' – as determined by psychiatrists and state authorities – can be connected to certain privileges. Apparent 'sanity' might be more accessible to people who experience more safety in the world – for example, because they are less likely to experience sexual violence. And for those deemed to have 'lost it', psychiatric intervention is often carceral.

Under powers afforded by the 1983 Mental Health Act (MHA), police may enter your home by force, physically restrain, arrest and lock you up, simply because they have decided that – as the NHS website puts it – you 'appear to have a mental disorder and are in need of immediate care or control'. In the Act, 'mental disorder' is defined vaguely as 'any disorder or disability of the mind'.

What the state's 'care or control' entails varies greatly depending upon the identity of the person concerned. Mental health 'care' for Black people is more likely to mean criminalisation. In 2020, Black people were four times more likely than white people to be detained or 'sectioned' under the MHA, and more likely to suffer poor treatment, abuse and even death whilst subject to psychiatric intervention and institutionalisation.

Detention under the MHA involves a near total removal of consent, including regarding the administration of medication, physical restraint and freedom of movement – often for years at a time. Psychiatric in-patients in NHS trusts can be subjected to 24/7 video surveillance without their consent.[35] In February 2022, a patient died in Huntercombe Hospital Maidenhead, a mental health facility for children and teenagers, following its being rated 'inadequate' by the Care Quality Commission in 2021, and repeated reports by patients of restraint that left them covered in bruises. Following the patient's death, a 17-year-old fellow patient started a petition calling for Huntercombe to be closed, describing 'staff negligence … enforced by management on a regular basis', causing 'innocent young children to die when they are in a place that is supposed to keep us alive'.[36]

People experiencing mental health crises can also be subjected to a controversial NHS programme called 'Serenity

Integrated Mentoring' (SIM),* which began expanding across the UK five years ago. A cost-saving measure designed by former police officer Paul Jennings, SIM intends to stop people in distress – often at high risk of self-harm or suicide – from calling upon emergency services. The programme coerces 'high intensity users' of emergency services into meeting with police officers, who are given access to their medical records. These officers are empowered to put pressure on patients to reduce their 'attention-seeking' use of public services such as ambulances, hospitals and mental health provision. If individuals do not comply, officers can threaten criminal sanctions, such as Community Behaviour Orders or prison. Most people subjected to this model are women who have been given the highly stigmatised diagnosis of 'borderline personality disorder', who are often survivors of complex trauma including sexual violence.

The diagnoses that attend psychiatric intervention are political. In the diagnostic process, some people's subjectivities are affirmed, whilst others' are denied, attacked or weaponised against them. Whilst queer people are less likely now than in the past to have their sexuality explicitly pathologised by a therapist, queer women, for example, are much more likely to be diagnosed with borderline personality disorder. Likewise, Black men are ten times more likely than white men to be diagnosed with psychosis.

In the mental health charity Mind's submission to the 2018 review of the MHA, a Black person with lived experience of the Act is quoted as saying: 'Racism is steeped deeply within British society and its institutional structures, including the

---

* At the time of writing, many mental health trusts have stopped using SIM thanks to resistance led by the StopSIM Coalition, a group of mental health service users, survivors and allies. However, mental health trusts still routinely collaborate with the police, and some are still running SIM-like programmes.

health service. A long history of slavery and colonialism shapes how Black people and other minorities are perceived and treated as variously dangerous, child-like, and intellectually inferior, which evokes at the very least a paternalism of "we know best".' [37] In reference to Community Treatment Orders – a controlling and punitive measure for previously sectioned people, dubbed 'psychiatric ASBOs' – the submission said that Black steering group members experienced the regime as 'coercive and intrusive while, at the same time, hugely unsupportive', with some seeing it as a form of 'race surveillance'.

Many people in severe mental distress, of course, are not detained in psychiatric wards where there is a veneer of 'treatment'. Especially if they are men – and even more likely if they are Black men – many are locked up in prisons, where suffering people are punished with more suffering. Whilst 'deviant women have been constructed as insane', wrote the political activist and scholar Angela Davis in *Are Prisons Obsolete?*, 'deviant men have been constructed as criminal'.[38]

Some such men in the UK today are shut away in so-called Close Supervision Centres (CSCs), a form of solitary confinement representing an even harsher version of the Special Security Units (SSUs) that Amnesty International has argued 'constitute cruel, inhuman or degrading treatment'.[39] Prisoners in CSCs – among whom self-harm and suicide rates are very high – are locked up for 23, sometimes 24, hours per day, and fed through a hatch. No contact is permitted with other prisoners, and they are escorted to exercise and showers by multiple guards in riot gear. The only established temporary exit for prisoners in CSCs is to be sectioned and sent to a high-security psychiatric hospital such as Broadmoor. Despite this, CSCs have been endorsed by the Royal College of Psychiatrists as being eligible for 'Enabling Environment' status, an award for services 'where everyone thrives, succeeds and achieves more positive outcomes'.[40]

Since incarceration exacerbates and precipitates mental illness, mental health practitioners are nowadays often brought into prisons to provide support - so the prison system claims. But prisoners and campaigners say mental health professionals' involvement often amounts to collusion with the system's attempts to control and punish vulnerable people. This claim has historical precedent; punitive psychiatry has always been used to dominate, delegitimise and lock up 'rebellious' people, including political dissidents. In 1851, for example, the American doctor Samuel A. Cartwright invented the diagnosis 'drapetomania' to describe the 'mental disorder' of enslaved Africans attempting to free themselves. More recently, as explored by the psychiatrist Jonathan Metzl in *The Protest Psychosis*, schizophrenia diagnoses have been used to repress Black militancy and defend white supremacy.[41]

Societies have long shunned and punished people judged to have transgressed norms of acceptable composure and descended into 'insanity'. In the 1970s, members of East London Big Flame, a revolutionary socialist feminist group, wrote in their Red Therapy pamphlet: 'Defining people as "mad" or "evil" as an excuse for putting them away or destroying them has been a common practice since the witches of the middle ages and before.'[42] In England, as early as the sixteenth and seventeenth centuries, 'houses of correction' were used to discipline poor people who were considered 'mad'. Ever since, institutionalisation and incarceration have been used as tools of power over those considered deviant, including those experiencing high levels of mental distress.

Anti-psychiatry and radical care

Psychiatric abuse led to the rise of the anti-psychiatry movement in the 1960s and '70s. The movement disavowed psychiatry's non-consensual use of drugs and violent 'treatments' such as electro-convulsive therapy, and critiqued its reliance on a medical model, considering mental distress only in terms of clinical diagnoses rather than as an experience arising in social contexts. The psychiatrist R. D. Laing – among the most recognised people associated with anti-psychiatry – believed that 'insanity' could instead be considered a sane response to an insane world.

In 1965, Laing co-founded a community house at Kingsley Hall in East London, aiming to provide an anti-authoritarian alternative to psychiatric hospitals, in a therapeutic home for mentally ill people, particularly those impacted by schizophrenia. As a brochure from the time explained, Kingsley Hall was 'a melting pot, a crucible in which many assumptions about normal–abnormal, conformist–deviant, sane–crazy experience and behaviour were dissolved. No person gave another tranquillisers or sedatives. Behaviour was feasible which would have been intolerable elsewhere. It was a place where people could be together and let each other be.'[43]

Since the inception of anti-psychiatry, propelled by the resistance of other liberation movements, 'survivor-led' and 'mad liberation' groups have proliferated, organising collectively for freedom from sanist oppression. In 1969, the People, Not Psychiatry (PNP) network was founded as a therapeutic alternative to institutionalised mental health interventions. PNP's first 'non-manifesto', published in the mid-1970s, introduced the network as follows:

It is people that are important; people, not psychiatry. And people need people; that is to say human beings cannot be fully human in isolation from other people … We meet each other as holistic beings, not as role players bearing such labels as Social Deviant, Psychotic, Psychiatrist, and so on. We accept each other as we are and for what we are, not for what we expect of each other. Everyone's experience and life-style is accepted as valid for them.[44]

'PNP House' was a squat, inspired by Kingsley Hall, where people in mental distress attempted to find respite and healing through communal living and mutual aid. Indeed, anti-psychiatry and mental health service user and survivor-led movements frequently overlap with other radical experiments and struggles. In the 1970s, the Red Lesbian Brigade – an autonomous group of Gay Liberation Front members – graffitied and flyered psychiatric hospitals, including the Maudsley in London, to protest the pathologisation of homosexuality and attendant conversion therapy. Their leaflets read:

WE ARE NOT SICK. WE ARE NOT ABNORMAL. WE ARE NOT IMMATURE.
Stop making a fat living out of saying we are.
WE ARE STRONG. WE ARE BEAUTIFUL. Power to the patients, we don't need you![45]

Today, mental health service user or survivor-led movements continue to fight for liberation. 'Recovery in the Bin' (RITB) is a critical theory and activism collective resisting the neoliberal medical model's co-option of 'recovery' as a method to control and discipline people experiencing mental distress. RITB believes that in a world of 'intolerable social and economic conditions, such as poor housing, poverty, stigma, racism, sexism, unreasonable work expectations, and countless other barriers',[46] meaningful 'recovery' is not always possible, or even desirable – at least in the terms set out by the medical model, which recognises only a narrow ideology of 'recovery' compatible with normative markers of success, according to which work is a moral standard.

The growing 'mad liberation' movement is abolitionist, often fighting in tandem with struggles against police, prisons and other forms of incarceration such as immigration detention and deportation. The Campaign for Psychiatric Abolition (CPA), for example, is 'a collective of psychiatric survivors fighting against the harm of psychiatry, policing and incarceration'.[47] Since psychiatry is tied up with the racist state and other forms of oppression inherent to the capitalist system such as transphobia, for the CPA psychiatric abolition is inextricably linked to anti-capitalism and liberation for all.

The CPA and other survivor-led groups often support Mad Pride, a movement reclaiming 'madness' from the clutches of pathologising discourses and disempowering psychiatric practices. Inspired by Gay Pride, Mad Pride marches aim to make the violence faced by mental health service users and psychiatric survivors visible. 'Bed push' actions, during which hospital beds are wheeled through public spaces, symbolise escape – the freeing of each other – from a carceral psychiatric system.

Mad Pride might also mean rethinking diagnoses. For example, as the author Meg-John Barker suggests, what was once known as 'multiple personality disorder' (now 'dissociative identity disorder') can be reconceived using queer theory and alternative therapeutic approaches such as transpersonal psychotherapy to celebrate, rather than problematise, plural and fluid experiences of self as common, if not universal, ways of being a person in the world.[48]

There are alternatives to the medical model, mainstream forms of therapy and institutionalisation for people experiencing emotional distress. Radical alternatives seek to recognise and address the causes of mental illness in the world, not only to remedy the symptoms, and to help people survive when conditional state support is either inaccessible, inadequate or retraumatising.

People at the sharp end of multiple forms of oppression demonstrate how community care, in everyday acts of embodied solidarity, keeps more people alive and more people well. The QueerCare network is a transfeminist autonomous care organisation providing training, support and advocacy for queer and trans people, aiming to build communities in which people know how to look after each other, with the necessary resources – from nutritious food to medical equipment to legal support. On the frontlines of patriarchal capitalism – facing stigma and exclusion in mainstream services, and state violence and criminalisation – sex workers too demonstrate the power of community care. Mutual aid among sex workers includes organising meet-ups to share information and resources; building community safety networks online; unionising to take back power from exploitative bosses; and starting hardship funds and workers' co-ops during times of crisis, as many sex worker groups – for example the Sex Worker Advocacy and Resistance Movement, and United Sex Workers – have done during the Covid-19 pandemic.

Whilst it is true that the concept of 'community' can be useful to capital – particularly with the idea that people should 'fill the gaps' of ever-disintegrating state support, as seen with the Tories' 'Big Society', an ideology premised on a neoliberal devolution of responsibility from the state to local communities – community care is vital, and the grassroots resilience and networks of interdependence it supports foment counter-power to the state that makes survival a struggle.

In an atomised and divided society, however, many people are not part of anything resembling 'community'. Fisher questioned the idealisation of the concept for this reason, instead proposing 'care without community', asking: 'Isn't that what we want? Where you can give people care regardless of whether they belong to the community?'[49] Radical care, then, could also be understood as 'collective', insisting upon well-being as a shared responsibility.

Therapeutic practices themselves can integrate liberatory values and approaches and be a part of political organising. For example, therapists in the Radical Therapist Network are committed to building 'intersectional, trauma informed, anti-racist, anti-capitalist and anti-oppressive therapeutic praxis', and have set up a fund to enable queer, trans and intersex Black people, Indigenous people and people of colour to receive free weekly talking therapy for a year, and to train therapist members 'to deliver intersectional, anti-oppressive, gender and sexuality affirming, trauma-informed, trans-cultural therapy with a particular focus on anti-racist and anti-capitalist therapeutic practice'.[50] Unlike many conventional approaches, such therapy necessarily pays attention to the material realities and positionalities of people's lives.

Therapy that supports liberation struggles breaks down hierarchy. Rather than the 'disordered' or 'sick' patient and the 'sane' or 'well' professional, the starting point might be: if one of us is suffering, we are all suffering. From feminist consciousness-raising groups, to men's groups, to group therapy, to co-counselling, experiments abound in therapeutic spaces that seek to both tug at the root causes of suffering as well as soothe its everyday aches.

An anti-capitalist politics of depression, Frantzen argues, must reject the 'neoliberal responsibilization of the depressed subject' and instead 'collectivize suffering, externalize blame, communize care'. Frantzen quotes Franco Berardi, who claims that 'in the days to come, politics and therapy will be one and the same'.[51] Indeed, paying attention to how psychotherapeutic concepts – such as repression, defence mechanisms, projection and repetition – show up at a societal level could bolster emancipatory struggles. And trying to comprehend and work through rather than deny our own insecurities, vulnerabilities and flaws is, at the very least, not amenable to the far right, which relies upon fantasies of supremacy and scapegoating – it could even be considered a kind of resistance.

In the 1970s, East London Big Flame members experimented with group therapy as a means of – and antidote to the difficulties involved in – doing radical politics together, including in the women's movement and housing activism. Their leaderless groups – some women's, some men's and some mixed gender – met regularly, acting as open forums for feelings, and sometimes they went on intensive, therapeutic weeks away. The groups sought to actively address intra-group power dynamics, and learned and shared their skills in therapeutic modalities such as co-counselling, guided fantasy, Gestalt, regression and somatic therapies such as massage. 'We see doing therapy, in the ways we want to do it, as part of the whole fight against capitalism's control over our lives', wrote the collective in the Red Therapy pamphlet where they documented their efforts. 'Therapy is much more than just making life tolerable so that we can fight better on other "fronts". It is part of the long-term struggle to reclaim our own emotional and personal resources.'[52]

Many groups today follow in the footsteps of such collaborative approaches to therapy. Hearts and Minds[*] is a peer support group holding London-based and online sessions by and for young people with lived experience of mental health struggles or emotional distress. The sessions are informed by the theory of 'intentional peer support', which focuses on the power of mutual, transformative relationships that support all people in the encounter to find new ways of thinking, seeing and doing. Ultimately, the group is interested in social change, with transformative therapeutic spaces underpinning the

[*] Now volunteer-run, due to lack of funding.

system overhauls necessary to address the reasons why many people experience mental distress.

Collective care beyond the state requires preparedness for mental health crises. Some radical mental health groups and therapeutic communities recommend creating crisis support plans. The Campaign for Psychiatric Abolition, for example, has written a document entitled 'How we can help each other during a mental health crisis'.[53] In defiance of the medical model, its advice is informed by the principle that a person in crisis knows best what will help them. An individual's crisis support plan might include known warning signs that they are approaching crisis point; important boundaries such as not contacting estranged family members; words or actions that can help ground them, including harm-reduction strategies; and named people or groups the crisis plan can be shared with. Such approaches aim to ensure people in extreme distress can be better supported by those around them, making institutionalisation – that could put them at risk of coercion, criminalisation and detention – less likely.

Radical therapy should be trauma-informed and based on values of transformative justice. This means acknowledging that people's feelings and behaviours are related to their past experiences, rather than a consequence of some inherent 'brokenness' or 'badness' – including when they act in very challenging or even harmful ways. Understanding does not mean excusing.

In *Detransition, Baby*, a novel by Torrey Peters, the protagonist Ames reflects upon how, during his final year living as a woman before detransitioning, he became 'sad and contemplative about how trans women treat each other'.[54] At the time, he recalls, his reflections were inspired by a (real) essay titled 'Elephant Breakdown' in the science journal *Nature*. The article shows how a period of exceptional cruelty and violence by some juvenile elephants in the Hluhluwe Imfolozi Game

Reserve in South Africa could be explained not, as previously thought, by high levels of testosterone or competition for resources, but, as Peters writes, by 'a form of chronic stress, a species-wide trauma that has led to a total and ongoing breakdown of elephant culture'.[55] All three of the elephants ravaging life around them were from an orphan generation; their elders had been mutilated and killed by humans, before their eyes. All three had once been chained to the bodies of their dead and dying kin.

Even in apparently radical approaches to care, the fact that lived trauma often begets inflicted trauma is rarely meaning-fully incorporated. This can be true of activist groups, too – including those with an apparent commitment to abolition-ist principles. Often, a carceral logic of 'care' – sometimes reiterating abuse through public harassment, shunning and punishment – takes the place of transformative approaches that leave space for people to take responsibility for their behaviours, and change. Surely, for any healing to happen, indeed for liberation to be possible, we must know ourselves and others to be both hurt and hurting, harmed and harmful – and to be fluid: always capable of being otherwise.

Well-being pending revolution

The softness of care rejects the hard systems that propagate suffering. Beyond vapid understandings of self-care and wellness, as defined by mostly rich white people, or forms of therapy that individualise suffering, we might find liberatory possibilities in looking after. It is most often people whose identities mean they fare relatively well in the world, and those unaccustomed to the feminised labour of caring, especially white cis straight men, who dismiss this idea as not urgent or necessary – not 'real' politics. Those subject to more systemic trauma and violence know better. As Lorde – a Black lesbian living with a cancer diagnosis – wrote: 'Caring for myself is not self-indulgence, it is self-preservation, and that is an act of political warfare.'[56] In another essay, Lorde suggests Black women 'can learn to mother ourselves', meaning: 'I affirm my worth by committing myself to my own survival.'[57]

Along with many other Black revolutionaries, Lorde insists upon the political power of caring for our own bodies and minds, and for those of our comrades. Political organising itself can be nurturing. From 1969, the Black Panther Party (BPP) in the United States ran 'survival programmes' – including free breakfasts for children, medical clinics, self-defence and first-aid classes, political education, transport to visit loved ones in prison, and addiction rehabilitation support. BPP co-founder Huey P. Newton described the rationale for these programmes as follows:

> We recognized that in order to bring the people to the level of consciousness where they would seize the time, it would be necessary to serve their interests in survival by developing programs which would help them to meet their daily needs ... All these programs satisfy the deep needs of the community but they are not solutions to our problems. That is why we call them survival programs, meaning survival pending revolution.[58]

In meeting people's needs, the BPP aimed not only to keep them alive and well, but 'to get them to understand the true reasons why they are in need in such an incredibly rich land',[59] so they might fight back. In this way, political organising – whether for quality social housing, for police abolition or against government cuts – can be both a way of improving material conditions, and a form of self- and collective care.

Fighting for the freedom to be well is not all about 'doing', however; sometimes it is about refusing to do what capitalism expects. For example, the Bare Minimum Collective – a group of Black feminists, queer theorists and creatives, many of whom are disabled – believes in 'doing nothing or at the very least, as little as is required of us'; 'space for pleasure'; and 'the abolition of everything but care, mutual aid and community'.[60] Either because our bodies won't allow us (because of disability, illness, exhaustion) to do 'more', or because we have conflicting responsibilities (in caring for others) or desires (for idleness, art, indulgence), sometimes resistance – or simply existence – means doing only what we need to do to stay and feel alive.

World-changing takes many forms. In *Sick Woman Theory*, Johanna Hedva proposes that for those who carry the trauma of 'our current regime of neoliberal, white-supremacist, imperial-capitalist, cis-hetero-patriarchy ... most modes of political protest are internalized, lived, embodied, suffering, and no doubt invisible'. They ask: 'How do you throw a brick through the window of a bank if you can't get out of bed?' Contrary to patriarchal conceptions of revolution, caring for ourselves and each other can be 'the most anti-capitalist protest', because:

> once we are all ill and confined to the bed, sharing our stories of therapies and comforts, forming support groups, bearing witness to each other's tales of trauma, prioritizing the care and love of our sick, pained, expensive, sensitive, fantastic bodies, and there is no one left to go to work, perhaps then, finally, capitalism will screech to its much-needed, long-overdue, and motherfucking glorious halt.[61]

We must collectively seize wellness as a common good – and reimagine it. We must recognise that suffering, and the resources to feel better, are unevenly distributed by design. Our hidden agonies can become fuel to burn it all down. We must rebuild by transforming the ways in which the world is psychically destructive and facilitates violence, and organise instead for communalised care. Our tending to each other will overcome alienation and galvanise resistance. We must imagine life beyond the lonely slog and find utopian moments of living otherwise that help us know it is possible. In seeking solace, let's give ourselves permission, as Kate Bornstein advises in *Hello, Cruel World: 101 Alternatives to Suicide for Teens, Freaks and Other Outlaws*, to do anything that makes life more worth living – whilst attempting to follow 'one simple rule: DON'T BE MEAN'.[62]

CHAPTER TWO

Us two against the world

Not gay as in happy, queer as in fuck your borders.
Lesbians and Gays Support the Migrants

Why two? Why two? I don't understand the two ... I think we should ask the question.
Judith Butler

Less than a year before his affair with adviser Gina Coladangelo was exposed by *The Sun* newspaper, former UK health secretary Matt Hancock failed to define an 'established relationship' live on television. The government's Covid-19 rules at the time allowed sex only in a relationship defined as such – which amounted, so Hancock's Sky News interviewer Kay Burley suggested, to a 'casual sex ban'.

Burley had two questions: When can people fuck freely? And what is an 'established relationship' anyway? Hancock could answer neither, but his flustered, labyrinthine responses were TV gold, and the dynamic between him and Burley made it seem like the sublimated question might be, when can *we* fuck? 'Why am I whispering? I don't know!' giggled Burley. 'I don't know, you're live on national TV, Kay', Hancock bantered. Burley teased him: 'It's okay to smile.'

The viral clip of their exchange – in which they attempt to delineate 'casual sex' from an 'established relationship' – is both a chronicle of governmental futility and circularity and a study in heteronormativity. As if cosplaying a beleaguered girlfriend, Burley asks stumped boyfriend Hancock what an 'established relationship' means *to him*. The two awkwardly agree that he is in such a relationship with 'Mrs Hancock'. ('I want you', a text message to a Covid-era lover might have read. 'I'm not sure we should', would read the disappointed reply. 'I just don't think we're "there" yet ... I mean, in a "Mr and Mrs Hancock relationship".')

Seeking specifics, Burley ventures whether 'established' might mean saying 'I love you' (but 'some people say that, and they don't mean it!'), or going out for dinner ('twice?'), or knowing each other for six months?

By those and many other standards, Hancock and Coladangelo's relationship, as well as his marriage, was surely 'established'. Yet CCTV footage of the pair's snatched snog and arse-squeezing prompted national, fascinated scandal. Rather than on account of his deadly mismanagement of the pandemic, Hancock resigned immediately after the affair became public.

Forsaking all others

Marriage rates in the UK for straight couples have never been lower,[1] and divorce rates continue to rise[2] – but the institution and its ostensible framework, monogamy, are still held dear in society. Infractions of this framework are generally seen as moral failings. Certainly, cheating – breaking an agreement of exclusivity in a relationship – involves betrayal and dishonesty; it can be traumatic and damage relationships. At the same time, the gravity ascribed to cheating compared to other determinants affecting the health of a relationship – such as open communication, emotional safety, mutual care and autonomy – is worth examining.

Despite Hancock's wife being a wealthy Conservative who had benefited from people's suffering under the cruel government policies imposed by the man she chose to marry, when she was cheated on her political affiliations suddenly mattered little even to some committed leftists. Sex 'as the root of virtue' has long been a 'special case' in our culture, wrote Susan Sontag, 'evoking peculiarly inconsistent attitudes'.[3] People of all political affiliations expressed compassion for Hancock's scorned wife, and lauded her for behaving with 'dignity'.

It is likely that Martha and Matt had not, in fact, agreed upon a non-monogamous marriage. The fact that we can be fairly sure about this speaks volumes to the enduring dominance of 'compulsory monogamy' – in which monogamy is not only assumed, but considered natural and right, and encouraged by societal forces, from pop songs to state policies promoting and rewarding marriage. After Hancock's shambolic television interview, a survey of British people showed that 70 per cent of respondents believed that being in an 'established relationship' meant being 'exclusive' (so neither of Hancock's relationships was established, in that case).[4]

Because of this 'compulsory' aspect, attempting to work out what we really want in relation to monogamy can be confusing – as a desire, it has been muddied by social pressure to comply and by institutionalisation. Heterosexuality, or alignment with its mores, is also 'compulsory' in this way. Adrienne Rich's concept of compulsory heterosexuality – or 'comphet' – explains how institutionalised heterosexuality is characterised by the 'absence of choice',[5] because of the psychological, cultural and material pressures that back it up whilst delegitimising and erasing lesbian experience. Meanwhile, consensually non-monogamous relationships are often delegitimised as, at best, kooky, slutty alternatives to 'real love' – or else as loveless, commitment-phobic aberrations threatening the sanctity of the couple form.

Public sex scandals might be less salacious if compulsory monogamy – like any dominant and institutionalised framework for sexuality – didn't predetermine relationships. If heterosexuality and monogamy are always already assumed – and assumed optimal – it can be difficult to do things differently, or even to imagine how they might be different, or admit we might want them to be. A well-known sexuality scholar once told me she was thinking of writing a book about how the prevalence of cheating can in part be explained by the barriers to expressing non-normative desires – but was scared off doing so by the fact she might be ostracised for 'defending cheaters', with the moral weight this carries.

With the protection of anonymity, however, in 2000, the decentralised anarchist collective CrimethInc published 'Adultery (and other half revolutions)'. The polemic considers whether – in a society where romantic love equals monogamy, 'desire is organized contractually' and anything else is considered 'bad ethics' – adultery could be understood as 'half a revolution'. The authors do not think cheating is good, or that it amounts to resistance against prevailing sexual mores. Instead, they describe it as 'the worst half' of the revolution, lacking in 'courage and analysis'. They propose that, rather than betraying and deceiving a lover, owning 'outlawed desires' and taking responsibility for the pain that might cause might go some way to resisting 'the circle of hurt that is the scarcity economy of love'.[6]

Is love a scarcity economy? In many ways, it isn't. People can and do proclaim to love multiple people (children, friends, family members). Only when it comes to romantic love do we contend with the truth claim that love is a zero-sum game.

Our current notion of romantic love has a short history. It was only in the seventeenth and eighteenth centuries that the idea of romantic love as the primary reason for marriage was explored – among the wealthy, in the West. Romantic love

44

as defined by sexual passion and intimate compassion was at this time a mostly extra-marital affair. It was not until the nineteenth century that 'love marriages' were more widely accepted, and even then marriage was ultimately a transaction – a matter of securing power within social groups by consolidating status, wealth and land, and preserving them in the hands of heirs. Women were thus traded on the marriage market as assets – mostly having little, if any, say in who they married.

Not so much has changed with regard to marriage as we might like to think. People still largely marry within their own race, religion and social class, influenced by family opinions. Most marriages retain elements of patriarchal ceremony: in a man asking a father for permission to 'take' his daughter's 'hand', for example, or in a woman being 'given away'. Research shows that whilst men married to women tend to be healthier and live longer, women married to men tend to die younger.[7] Whilst marriage or other commitment rituals need not be this way, it is important, as bell hooks argues, 'to have a sharp, ongoing critique of marriage in a patriarchal society – because once you marry within a society that remains patriarchal, no matter how alternative you want to be within your unit, there is still a culture outside you that will impose many, many values on you whether you want them to or not'.[8]

In *The Origin of the Family, Private Property and the State*, Friedrich Engels explores the history of the bourgeois 'monogamous family' as a way of organising society, explaining its purpose: to optimise private wealth accumulation and patrilineal property inheritance.[9] The 'monogamous family', as Engels construes it, was since its inception a unit to privatise care, transmit property and maximise consumption. A similar analysis has been applied to coupledom. 'The logic of the couple', argue Clémence x. Clémentine and associates from the Infinite Venom Girl Gang, is 'that which funnels, simplifies, and reduces amorous desire to the needs of patriarchy within the capitalist mode of production'.[10] With people relating primarily in twos, populations are also probably easier to control – and less likely to build power against the state – than would be the case if making more expansive intimate commitments were the norm.

By the mid-nineteenth century, monogamous marriage and the nuclear family were considered working-class aspirations, rather than solely the reserve of the rich. Those who adopted these forms, as the writer ME O'Brien argues, could access 'the narrow respectability of legal marriage' by differentiating themselves from the sex-working and queer 'deviants' of their class.[11]

In 'civilising missions', coloniser nations sought to supplant existing Indigenous forms of kinship – as well as less binary ways of doing gender and sexuality – with the 'respectable' form. This 'settler sexuality' – a 'heteropatriarchal and sexual modernity exemplary of white settler civilization', as the gender studies professor Scott L. Morgensen puts it[12] – was violently imposed on colonised peoples because it furthered imperial capitalist ends. 'Anti-sodomy laws' were introduced by colonial penal codes, and Indigenous peoples were often coerced into Christian marriage. As scholar and artist Leanne Betasamosake Simpson writes:

Since Michi Saagiig Nishnaabeg nationhood is at its core relational, and all of our political practices stem from the establishment and maintenance of good relations, Indigenous forms of social kinship had to be destroyed and replaced with the heteronormative nuclear families. Indigenous intimate partnerships were diverse and shattered the heteronormative sexual and relationship orientations of settlers. There were practices of nonmonogamy, separation, divorce, and situations where both genders had more than one partner. These unchurched relationships were the subject of much settler surveillance.[13]

The colonial imposition of settler sexuality was not total. In a 1978 essay on Black women and love, Audre Lorde writes that the Fon of Dahomey on the West Coast of Africa 'still have twelve different kinds of marriage, [including] where a woman of independent means marries another woman, who then may or may not bear children, all of whom will belong to the bloodline of the first woman'. This accepted kind of marriage, she says, is 'arranged to provide heirs for women of means who wish to remain "free", and some are lesbian relationships'.[14]

With reference to colonisation in North America – where Indigenous peoples traditionally practised more expansive forms of kinship such as extended kin groups, including plural marriage – Indigenous scholar Kim TallBear explains how and why settler forms were enforced:

If Indians could not all be killed outright ... then the savages might also be eliminated by forced conversions to whiteness ... both the church and the state evangelized marriage, nuclear family, and monogamy. These standards were simultaneously lorded over Indigenous peoples as an aspirational model and used to justify curtailing their biological reproduction and steal[ing] their children.

So marriage was yoked together with private property in settler coercions of Indigenous peoples. The breakup of Indigenous peoples' collectively held-lands into privately-held allotments controlled by men as heads-of-household enabled the transfer of 'surplus' lands to the state and to mostly European or Euro-American settlers.[15]

Racist disciplining of romantic and sexual intimacies also impacted former slaves in the United States. As outlined by O'Brien, Black proletarians during Reconstruction:

> seized on their freedom in forming new families and sexual relationships, drawing on the diversity of romantic codes forged under slavery. In government records gathered about black families after the American Civil War, historians find a diversity of relationship and family structures greater than their white contemporaries on farms or in factories. Many black couples during Reconstruction 'took up', in 'sweetheart' or 'trial marriages', or were 'living together' in non-marital, temporary and often non-monogamous romantic relationships. Couples could co-parent in such temporary arrangements, raising 'sweetheart children'.[16]

Where colonial and antebellum laws banned marriage between slaves, legal marriage was mandated for Black couples after the Civil War – and soon, O'Brien notes, 'black people were being investigated and prosecuted for violating marital laws' prohibiting fornication and adultery.[17]

Throughout history, laws regulating intimate relationships, especially marriage laws, have been about nation-building – whether by promoting white population growth over Black (for example in prohibitions of Black and interracial marriage), or by bringing previously excluded groups into the state-sanctioned kinship forms of marriage and the nuclear family (for example in legalising gay marriage).

The way the state and social norms construct sexuality is conceptualised by Christopher Chitty, in his book on 'statecraft, sodomy, and capital in the rise of the world system', as 'sexual hegemony': where the sexual norms – as 'aspirational fantasy' or 'a form of social status' – of a dominant group are naturalised to the extent that they shape the sexual behaviour and self-understanding of other groups. Sexual hegemony, argues Chitty, operates in inconsistent ways over time, is variably achieved by 'force and consent, repression and persuasion', and is a critical tool for the accumulation of capital and the consolidation of bourgeois rule.[18]

Are you on the market?

Most people don't think about their love lives in terms of capitalism, but how we practise and speak about such relationships is revealing. If we do not have a partner, we are 'on the market' – perhaps 'hot property' or, if we are an older woman, 'on the shelf'. Dating is competitive and involves investments; people's worth and value to us is weighed up as we 'shop around'. The logic of capitalism is rife in normative approaches to what might be among our most intimate relationships.

People are increasingly meeting romantic prospects using online platforms – or 'dating products' – owned by tech corporations such as Match Group, whose tagline promises 'Global Presence. Revolutionary Technology. Deeper Connections'. Match Group owns nearly every major US dating site, including Hinge, OkCupid and Tinder – the latter of which generated $1.4 billion in revenue in 2020, up from $47 million in 2015.

Dating apps require self-commodification – to optimise your 'assets' in competition with others. And whilst the internet can make dating more accessible for those who face more barriers to meeting people in person, discrimination rooted in oppressive systems plays out on the platforms. In quick-fire, anonymous swiping, perhaps it is even amplified. People who are racialised, trans, disabled or fat report facing repeated rejection or fetishisation on dating apps. The apps themselves can facilitate this. Multiple dating sites allow users to filter based on ethnicity, for example – and although the attendant bias is usually only said to *reflect* societal racism, this argument, as lecturer in digital media, culture and technology Alfie Bown notes, circumvents 'the possibility that [the apps'] own algorithms might be at least partially responsible for not only proliferating but re-writing sectarian trends in relationship building'.[19]

Apps are just one element of the dating industrial complex. For men who feel they need intensive 'rebranding' to be attractive romantic candidates for women, the industry offers a costly solution: pick-up artistry. Pick-up artist (PUA) coaching goes far beyond sharing flirting tips between friends. A day-long 'Impactful Connection' workshop in London led by PUA Johnny Cassell costs £750, and includes training on 'how to create solid high value social circles from scratch' and 'leverage' them for dating success, as well as fostering 'nightlife dominance' to 'pick up dancers and models'.[20] From 9 p.m. till midnight, course attendees access 'the real learning': a night out harassing women.

On Johnny Cassell's website there is a chat box. I ask the interface if there is any proof that the course will increase my chances of sleeping with beautiful women, and am told to look at the course's feedback testifying to its success rate for men seeking 'a higher calibre of woman'. The person messaging asks me if I have other goals. I want a good wife, I respond, not a feminist who refuses her duties. 'I certainly think we can help you', he types.

Cassell's course is subtler than some. Another PUA course – that of Nick Krauser – advertises access to 'younger, hotter, tighter' women through a five-day course costing £5,000. Krauser's FAQ page answers 'Yes' to 'Are you racist / sexist / homophobic?' Men fawn in the comments of his YouTube channel: 'When I grow up, I want to be just like you!!'[21]

Cassell's and Krauser's ideas about dating form part of the 'manosphere', an online misogynist, alt-right-adjacent community of mostly white men, where radicalisation can manifest in anti-feminist terrorism. Among this community are 'incels' – involuntary celibates – who pontificate in forums about why women won't have sex with them and develop theories about the dominant sexual order, in which only some people can be sexually 'successful'. Increasingly, incels are murdering women over this perceived injustice. In August 2021, Jake Davison, a 22-year-old white man from Plymouth who was active in the manosphere, killed five people in Britain's most deadly mass shooting in more than a decade.

The ideology that inspired this massacre is arguably an extremist version of that which guides heteronormative dating and sexual relations under capitalism. If romantic intimacy and sex are something to be 'won', and women are rendered property, commodified with varying degrees of 'value', then – according to this schema – some men are going to be 'losers'. In this worldview, as the writer Rebecca Solnit argues, for men, sex with 'high value' women can be a matter of primitive accumulation and status.[22] Being unable to accrue such status might lead to internalised disappointment or depression – or, it might result in men violating or killing women, who they see as the objects of their unfulfilled entitlement. The tragic irony of incel philosophy, as the philosopher Amia Srinivasan points out, is that the sexual order in which these men experience themselves as undesirable is the same culture of discrimination and objectification they are reiterating by demanding their 'right to sex' with only 'fuckable' – young, conventionally attractive, white, non-disabled, cis – women.[23]

Romance, sex and the state

The belief held by incels that their lives are futile without romantic relationships and sex is supported by the state's interventions in this arena. At school, children are taught both implicitly and explicitly the 'right and proper' behaviours in this realm. The dominant messaging: straight is good, marriage is the best. Indeed, mainstream sex education is not free from the legacy of Thatcher's Section 28, which banned schools and local authorities from 'promoting the teaching of the acceptability of homosexuality as a pretended family relationship'. The law was only revoked in 2000 in Scotland, and in 2003 in the rest of the UK. The latest UK relationships and sex education guidance places emphasis on marriage as a primary, lifelong commitment between two people, without including content about alternative forms.[24] The prevailing state agenda with regards to sex education is much more about upholding patriarchal morality than consent and pleasure.

Marriage is a privileged form of relationship, entailing social status as well as material benefits. The institution is commonly endorsed by religious leaders and politicians as the 'bedrock of our society' – ostensibly meaning a *moral* foundation, but also accurately describing the nuclear family's role for capitalism. The 'bedrock of our society' accolade has been invoked by Conservatives when legalising 'same-sex marriage', and when launching tax policies that incentivise marriage. Offering married couples tax breaks, said Prime Minister David Cameron in 2015, is about 'valuing commitment', because 'it's families who raise our children, look after our old and keep our country going'. Today, the 'marriage allowance' – which is only available to cohabiting couples who are married or in a civil partnership – reduces tax by around £250 a year.

Stigma around separation and divorce – especially without grave incompatibility or betrayal – persists. When Hancock's affair surfaced, the *Evening Standard Magazine* ran an editorial warning of the perils of leaving your spouse. The public infidelity should provide women with a 'lightening rod', it reads, suggesting they might clutch 'their messy, irritating husbands tighter' – because 'unless your partner is an abuser, a relationship is a relationship is a relationship, and swapping a dull one for a shiny new one can be a naïve mistake'.[25] While this statement is certainly not untrue – an enduring partnership must surely withstand boredom – the underlying assumption seems to be that mature love always means monogamy, and that a 'compare the market'-type approach can be mapped onto love and desire.

The promotion of marriage is entwined with reactionary politics. In 2018, the Conservative MP Derek Thomas proposed a parliamentary debate entitled 'Marriage and Government Policy'. Thomas, a former property developer and a supporter of evangelical Christian doctrines, scheduled the debate ahead of 'Marriage Week'. 'Marriage Week' is organised by the Marriage Foundation, which was set up by the High Court family judge Paul Coleridge, who has compared single parents to 'cancerous cells' in society,[26] and has links to the Christian right group Christian Concern, which is homophobic and anti-abortion. The Marriage Foundation – employing a common tactic of Christian right organisations in the United States – underpins its pro-marriage campaigning with unsubstantiated evidence of its quantifiable superiority as a way of life 'for the good of society … especially our children'.[27]

The belief that monogamous marriage and the nuclear family are superior ways of life is not supported by any meaningful evidence – yet the idea has been backed by successive governments. Finding somewhere to live is generally made easier for couples and 'families'. When registering for social housing, for example, couples who are married or in civil partnerships are prioritised for joint tenancies. 'We will not agree to an existing tenant having a joint tenancy with anyone other than a husband, wife, registered civil partner or partner', states one local authority website.[28] It is easier to rent a property as a nuclear family of five than as a group of five people who consider themselves 'family', because the law would not consider them one 'household' but a 'house share' – adverts often explicitly state, 'no sharers, families only'. In a particularly stark example of regulating intimacy, this year the city of Shawnee in Kansas, United States banned 'co-living' – meaning four or more unrelated people renting a home – altogether. And whilst home ownership is increasingly out of reach for a large section of society, two incomes can help, and buying 'as a couple', especially a married couple, entails more legal and financial protections. Buying a house as a group or as part of a cooperative structure is made very complicated by the law and banks.

When assessing people for benefits, the state assumes that someone with a 'partner' who has more money or resources can depend upon them for material support. Where someone is deemed to have a partner and 'the couple' is deemed eligible for benefits, those payments go into one person's account. This results in people being denied the state support they require, and traps them in relationships they may want to leave or need to leave for their safety.

For its own ends, the state seeks to categorise human relationships even though their forms are infinite. When a friend of mine tried to claim housing benefit whilst living with her close friend, she had to convince the government that he was not, in fact, her 'partner', which would have disqualified her from state support. What determines this, as Matt Hancock and Kay Burley grappled with, is anyone's guess. Interrogating my friend on the status of her domestic relationship, the interviewer asked whether the man she lived with made her tea, and where they sat when they got home from work.

Monogamy is a given in the state-sanctioned ideal of romantic relationships – despite the fact it was only from around the nineteenth century that monogamy became an expectation, at least, of men as well as women. A 2018 House of Commons briefing paper on polygamy states: 'In order to be recognised as legally valid, all marriages which take place in the United Kingdom must be monogamous.'[29] In theory, this means that legal marriage in the UK must be between two people, but the literal implications of the statement raise more questions. Monogamy is more commonly understood as sexual exclusivity between two people. According to this understanding, would every marriage that has involved cheating, and every marriage that is consensually non-monogamous, be legally invalid?

Meanwhile, until 1991, rape within marriage was not a criminal offence, a wedding apparently signifying ongoing consent to sex for life. A 1992 report for Parliament by The Law Commission paints a troubling picture of marriage. Most of the Criminal Law Revision Committee at the time did not consider 'non-consensual intercourse within marriage to be as grave an offence as non-consensual intercourse outside marriage'.[30] The report also debated the impact of criminalising marital rape on 'the parties' marriage and the institution of marriage'.[31]

'Adultery', on the other hand, in the UK and elsewhere, has long been considered an offence (even a crime) worthy of violent punishment – especially for women, though also for men who have sex with other men's wives. As the psychotherapist Esther Perel notes, adultery 'is the only commandment that is repeated twice in the Bible: once for doing it, and once for just thinking about it'.[32] In 1707, English Lord Chief Justice John Holt pronounced that a man having sex with someone else's wife was 'the highest invasion of property' and that 'a man cannot receive a higher provocation'. In many ways, prevailing sentiments haven't changed all that much today.

Whilst cheating isn't illegal in the UK today, is it for the most part considered unequivocally 'wrong' – in heterosexual relationships, often with different implications for men versus women. Infidelity is often invoked in legal proceedings as a justification for violent 'crimes of passion' – usually of men defending their 'honour' – and sometimes still results in lenient sentences or even exoneration. 'Provocation' as a mitigating legal defence for murder, which included 'a husband discovering his wife in the act of adultery', was only repealed in 2010, and it is still possible for judges to interpret defences related to infidelity from the succeeding defence, renamed 'loss of control'. In 2012, the UK's most senior judge ruled that juries should be allowed to consider adultery as provocation for murder, leading to Jon-Jacques Clinton, who killed his wife in their home, having his murder conviction quashed.*

Until April 2022, married people had to make accusations against each other in order to be granted a divorce.** Before 'no fault' divorce became legal at this time, 'adultery' was the first reason listed on the UK government's website as 'grounds for divorce'. 'Committing adultery', it specified, means: 'Your husband or wife had sexual intercourse with someone else of the opposite sex.'[33] A spouse having sex with someone who is not of the 'opposite sex' was not, then, considered cheating by the courts. Because heterosexist society does not consider queer sex 'real sex'? Because queer people are characterised as sexually promiscuous? Yes – but also because divorce law had not been updated since 1973, when gay sex between men was barely legal.***

---

* He was later convicted in a retrial.

** On 6 April 2022, 'no fault' divorce was introduced in England and Wales.

*** In 1967 in England and Wales, sex between two men over 21, in private, was legalised. The reform was not extended to Scotland until 1980, and to Northern Ireland until 1982. Despite this, many facets of queer life and sex remained criminalised decades later – gay sex between more than two people, or gay sex with more than two people present, for example, were only decriminalised in 2003.

But whilst adultery might not exist for 'same-sex' couples in UK law, marriage does. The fight for 'marriage equality' was finally won in 2014 in Britain, and in 2020 in Northern Ireland. Whilst the extension of the right to marry was widely celebrated, the issue was more contentious within the gay and queer liberation movement. To some, focusing on the right to marry was a concession to assimilation into ritualised, institutionalised – normal and therefore supposedly moral – heterosexual life. This trajectory, argues Michael Warner in his book *The Trouble with Normal*, not only distracts from more urgent arenas of oppression such as the poverty and violence queer people face, but shores up the dominant heteropatriarchal order in which many lives and relationships that cannot or will not be subsumed into a normative framework will always be marginalised, disposable and stigmatised as immoral.

On this issue, Warner quotes the conservative writer and activist Jonathan Rauch, who has advocated for same-sex marriage. Rauch argues in favour of gay marriage as a means of solidifying the privileged status of marriage in society, writing that 'it must be understood to be better, on average, than other ways of living … If gay marriage is recognized, single gay people over a certain age should not be surprised when they are disapproved of or pitied. That is a vital part of what makes marriage work. It's stigma as social policy.'[34] As Prime Minister David Cameron said in 2011: 'I don't support gay marriage despite being a Conservative. I support gay marriage because I'm a Conservative.'

Support for gay rights has been cast in 'homonationalist' terms, in which Western society is depicted as progressive, while migrants and racialised people – especially Muslims – are deemed exceptionally homophobic. This ahistorical position – ignoring the history of colonisation in which Western countries imposed anti-queer laws in the Global South – is then used to justify anti-migrant and racist opinions and policies, including military intervention.

Gay marriage – 'constructed as a kind of love marriage *par excellence*' – argues Sita Balani in her article 'What's Love Got to Do with It? Marriage and the Security State', has become a means by which the nation state, and specifically the UK, maintains a moral economy in which the normative discourse of romantic love can be held up against 'bad immigrants' and their arranged marriages.[35] Under the guise of a concern for women's welfare, freedom and the self-actualising status of romantic love – values that are attractive in the liberal imaginary – she argues, 'the wrong kind of marriage' is used as a straw man to justify racist borders.

This narrative is employed in attempts to stop 'sham marriages' – that is, marriages with the purpose of obtaining a visa. The state adjudicates on relationships and sexuality by subjecting migrants to intrusive, offensive and absurd interrogations by the Home Office, designed to reveal that their claim to 'real' love (and/or queerness) is a 'sham'. The idea that visa marriages are illegitimate rests on the idea that 'real' marriages are always motivated by a specific, organic and universal experience of romantic love – which of course is not the case, nor was it assumed to be the case in even recent history.

The state's arbitration on our romantic and sexual lives is backed up by a cultural, ideological system that deems some kinds of people and relationships 'good', 'normal' and 'natural' – indeed, more 'real' – and others 'bad', 'abnormal' and 'unnatural'. In her 1984 essay *Thinking Sex*,[36] Gayle Rubin conceptualised this 'sexual stratification' as a way in which society displaces social anxieties, especially during times of intense crisis – often through appeals, like that of the Marriage Foundation, to 'protect children' from imagined threats.

Good sex, according to Rubin's 'Charmed Circle' diagram, is heterosexual, monogamous, marital, reproductive, intragenerational and non-commercial; it happens at home, without porn, sadomasochism or sex toys. In the hierarchy of good to bad sex, she observes, 'Individuals whose behaviour stands high ... are rewarded with certified mental health, respectability, legality, social and physical mobility, institutional support, and material benefits', whilst those who 'fall lower on the scale ... are subjected to a presumption of mental illness, disreputability, criminality, restricted social and physical mobility, loss of institutional support, and economic sanctions'.[37]

The idea that a monogamous marriage or romantic partnership is more valuable than other kinds of relationships – sometimes called 'couple privilege' – was reinforced during the Covid pandemic and successive lockdowns. If you were involved in this kind of relationship you were encouraged to domesticate, and eventually granted visitation rights. If you were not in this kind of relationship – whether 'single' or in another kind of committed relationship – government policy signalled that your intimate life was immaterial.

As the writer Ben Weil argued during the pandemic, 'the UK government has heralded asceticism ... as the gold standard of public health',[38] as opposed to condoning 'safer' pandemic practices. Covid guidelines and legislation impacting people's relationships flew in the face of evidence from the AIDS crisis, which showed that disavowing sex outside of monogamous coupledom was not an effective strategy for sustainably reducing infection rates. Rather, writes Weil, insisting upon 'life-enhancing, community-building pleasure'[39] as vital was central to gay men's approach to developing the life-saving techniques we now understand as 'safer sex'.

The Covid-19 pandemic was harnessed as an opportunity to intensify what the writer Sophie Lewis has termed our 'collective turn-off'.[40] 'Erotophobia', she observes, runs deep both in the capitalist system and among its detractors. Boredom or a lack of pleasure, in our culture, are largely not acceptable reasons to end romantic relationships, nor to change their form. Indeed, if it disrupts our conformity to 'the way things are done' – in work, in public, at home, in relationships – transforming any element of our lives because of erotic or spiritual stagnation is often frowned upon. 'The denial of pleasure to populations is a grave historic harm', writes Lewis, 'and the denial by some leftists of the centrality of pleasure to liberation struggles is a correspondingly serious error'.[41]

If we are not finding pleasure in romantic coupledom – or indeed in our lives – the dominant cultural messaging holds: work harder. There are whole industries – in self-help, therapy and advice-giving – that profit from this ideal, generally exhorting heteronormative mores. The problem with this, argues Moira Weigel in *Labour of Love*, is not that we should expect relationships to be effortless, but that this 'relationship work' falls mostly on women, and individualises experiences and feelings that often reflect social forces.[42] The 'work', too, is often directed towards ends that we don't – so we might discover, if we dared – actually desire. The irony of the common-sense approach to romantic love, that positions it as everyone's highest aspiration, is that it doesn't really believe in the power of love. Whilst love might be a creative and transformative force, the logic of romantic love just exhorts us to comply to pre-written rules.

Longing for something 'more' or 'different' in a romantic relationship is often framed as naïve and selfish – a way of thinking that extends to common perceptions of bisexuality. This argument is almost always a defence of the couple form – of its integrity and longevity, regardless of the fulfilment or desires of its component humans. This isn't an anti-individualism, pro-communality position, but one that seeks to protect coupledom as a dominant social form at the expense of other possibilities for intimacy. This prioritisation of the couple form might involve a shrinking not only of the self, but also of more expansive intimacies – and therefore solidarities.

In Torrey Peters' novel *Detransition, Baby*, the character Katrina tells her partner Ames that she divorced her husband because of 'the ennui of heterosexuality'.[43] But because being bored is not deemed a good enough reason to justify ending a marital relationship, she tells him that she uses her miscarriage to explain the divorce. Later, when pregnant and meeting Reese – Ames' ex-partner with whom she, along with Ames, is considering raising the baby – Reese tells her that 'divorced cis women are my favourite people on earth'. More specifically: 'The ones who have seen how the narratives given to them since girlhood have failed them, and who know there is nothing to replace it all. But who still have to move forward without investing in new illusions or turning bitter – all with no plan to guide them.' These cis women, she says, are 'as close to a trans woman as you can get'.[44]

The myth that there is no alternative to the prevailing romantic and sexual order is confirmed all around us – in pop songs, in advertising, on reality television. On the dating game show *Love Island*, conventionally attractive men and women 'graft'* to win the status of being 'coupled up'. It could be 'a situationist intervention about comp-het',[45] writes Lewis; or, as the writer Rosanna McLaughlin suggests, it could be called 'straight camp'.[46] The programme, however, exposes the incongruity of desire with dogma.

Love Islanders worship a certain denomination of love. As Simon May contends in *Love: A History*, romantic love has acquired a God-like significance in societies bereft of spirituality and superstition. 'In the wasteland of Western idols', he writes, 'only love survives intact.'[47] Indeed, *Love Island*-love demands this religiosity overcome cognitive dissonance.

---

* On *Love Island*, contestants use 'graft' to refer to seduction attempts.

'Islanders' declare their faith that the competition will result in till-death romantic partnerships, against all the odds of the show's archives; contestants are apparently evangelical about 'real love' being monogamous, whilst *Love Island*'s premise depends upon their multiple, often simultaneous, attractions and affections.

Every year, *Love Island* involves a 'test' in which the men and women who have formed couples are split up and rehoused – in Casa Amor – with a new set of people of the 'opposite sex'. The idea is to 'test' whether the couples' monogamy – seemingly assumed rather than agreed upon – can endure each of them meeting new people. If they fail the test, it follows, maybe they didn't really like each other after all. Contestant Millie, worrying about whether the man she is 'coupled up' with, Liam, is attracted to another woman in Casa Amor, describes the stakes as: 'whether or not what we had was real, or if it was just a complete load of crap'. When Millie is reunited with Liam and discovers he has kissed another woman, she is understandably hurt. His behaviour, she believes, signals that he must not have strong feelings for her, which he contests.

If a cheater explains their straying because of an already failing relationship, this fits 'the logic of romance narrative',[48] observes Berlant. If they maintain that both relationships are valuable and independent of each other, the adulterer adopts 'the logic of fantasy, protecting all positions as sites of her own desire'.[49] Neither position is false, argues Berlant, because each is 'affectively true' to different people. *Love Island*'s Liam takes a different approach, retorting: 'If you were my girlfriend, I wouldn't have even *looked* at anyone else.' This, says Millie, was already her position. 'I didn't even fucking get to know anyone', she tells him of her own Casa Amor experience, to which he responds: 'That means the world to me, it does.'

The belief that honouring a monogamous partnership means shutting down or shrinking even non-sexual intimacies with other people is commonplace, and one aspect of what has been termed 'toxic monogamy'.* In toxic monogamy, romantic relationships are supposed to be our all-encompassing source of meaning and fulfilment: partners should spend most of their time together and meet all each other's needs; attraction to other people should cease (sexual exclusivity is essential, jealousy indicates love); self-worth is to be found in one's worth to the other; and love should conquer all incompatibilities. An example of 'toxic monogamy' might be the celebrities' Megan Fox and Machine Gun Kelly's engagement, which made the headlines in 2022: he proposed using a ring designed with thorns, such that it would hurt if she tried to take it off. If monogamy and marriage are enshrined in this way, it is little wonder the tagline for hen and stag dos is 'last night of freedom'.

In many cases, this entails the 'freedom' not only to have sex with other people, but to share emotional intimacy with them – especially with people of genders you might conceivably want to have sex with. The website for Relate, the UK's largest provider of relationship counselling, states that having an 'emotional affair' might involve being 'excited about talking to' someone, sharing news with them 'before telling your partner', and enjoying 'emotional attention and interest'.[10]

Even though cultural artefacts like *Love Island* frequently demonstrate the challenges and contradictions of normative scripts, it is inconceivable that they would allow for conclusions that might bring those scripts into question. After all, the success of such products rests upon – as Berlant puts it – 'the

---

* Attributed to Hillary Berry, though her original article 'Toxic Monogamy Culture' is no longer available online.

logic of romance narrative'. Since this logic can only accommodate certain affective realities, it necessarily forecloses the possibility of other ways of being.

Sara Ahmed considers this in relation to the compulsion to be happy about weddings, on which £14.7 billion is spent every year in the UK. 'How quickly we learn: for the child, especially the girl child, her happiest day will be the moment of marrying',[51] she writes, observing that this 'will be' is not only a prediction, but 'a moral instruction' that begins in childhood, when heterosexuality is presumed. If a woman is unhappy on her wedding day, it follows, she becomes 'an affect alien': 'not made happy by the right things'.[52] Being an 'affect alien' – experiencing what Arlie Russell Hochschild terms 'inappropriate affect'[53] – can be lonely or painful. 'Inappropriate affect' – including but not only in the sphere of romantic relationships and sex – is, as such, often the source of shame, repressed in ourselves and policed in others. Smile! It's your wedding day!

The dominant romantic and sexual order chimes with how many people experience their desires. Then again, our desires are shaped by our contexts, and when certain desires are 'compulsory' it can be difficult to tune into what could, possibly, feel like more authentic ways of being. In our sex lives, as observed by Katherine Angel in *Tomorrow Sex Will be Good Again*, patriarchal scripts and sexual violence, along with the pressure that 'empowered' women should be able to enthusiastically proclaim their sexual desires, can make it difficult for women to know what they want – or to embrace the unknowability and everchanging nature of desire.[54]

When certain ways of feeling and being are privileged – entailing social and material rewards, often as opposed to judgement and punishments – consent is called into question. We do not live in a consensual world. 'Non-consent is normalised at every level', writes Meg-John Barker in their

'Consent Checklist': in the 'wider culture, our institutions and communities, our interpersonal relationships and everyday interactions, and within ourselves (self-consent)'.[55] And if the alternative to the normative vision for romantic relationships is pitched as 'dying alone' – as described by many existential dread-filled memes – how possible is it to imagine, let alone consider and practise, other options without fear?

Sex and revolution

Expanding the realm of the possible in our thinking about romantic relationships and sex has much to recommend it. It is widely accepted that more freedom in this sphere up until now has been a positive. Though the horizon of liberation remains far off, gay relationships, for example, are today less persecuted than they were, and unmarried women and single mothers are subject to less discrimination than before. Despite this, even on the left, it can be hard to convince people that much *more freedom* is necessary. Conversations relating to intimate relationships and sex can evoke peculiarly defensive responses.

Indeed, conflicts over sex often spill over into societal-level politics in 'moral panics'.

As observed by Rubin, these panics are never about what they claim to be: 'Because sexuality in Western societies is so mystified, the wars over it are often fought at oblique angles, aimed at phony targets, conducted with misplaced passions, and are highly, intensely symbolic. Sexual activities often function as signifiers for personal and social apprehensions to which they have no intrinsic connection.'[56] For example, the 'sex wars' of the 1970s and '80s, in which feminists battled over the meaning of pornography, sex work and sadomasochism; and the intense homophobia whipped up during the HIV/AIDS crisis. Often, 'protecting the children' is invoked to displace fear and hate. At the 1987 Conservative Party Conference, Margaret Thatcher warned that 'children who need to be taught to respect traditional moral values are being taught that they have an inalienable right to be gay'. Today, we see this rhetoric being used in attempts to justify transphobic views.

Moral panics reveal sublimated anxieties. If women are allowed to petition for divorce on equal terms, my wife might leave me for another man! If gay people are allowed marriages, it might change the significance of my straight one! If some relationships are non-monogamous, my monogamous one might be threatened! People often find reasons to negate increasing freedoms in the intimate sphere – intentionally or unintentionally shoring up the status quo – because, on some level, we are scared that a widening of acceptable ways of being might challenge the validity or stability of the identities and relational forms in which we seek meaning and security. Moral panic might take the form of, say, launching a 'Marriage Foundation', or refusing to bake pro-gay marriage cakes.* Or, it could take the shape of feminists attending conferences attempting to mastermind trans-exclusionary politics, or people demeaning polyamory on Twitter.

Berlant defines 'the phobic' as 'those who fear instabilities of privilege and embrace the social as a site of sameness'. In the phobic imagination, she argues, 'non-normative sexualities threaten fantasies of the good life that are anchored to images of racial, religious, class, and national mono-culture'.[57] We are all, in one way or another, phobic; dismantling the ways that we are is lifelong work. It isn't simply possible, by making certain choices, to 'opt out' of the ways in which the dominant logic of romance and sex is oppressive. To a large extent, the

---

* In 2014, Ashers bakery in Northern Ireland refused to bake a cake iced with the slogan 'Support Gay Marriage'.

systems we live in under capitalism predetermine the possible – possible thoughts, feelings, desires and ways of relating. But we can, at least, try to become conscious of the ways we have internalised the dominant culture, and ask ourselves what this might mean for our lives.

In progressive political movements today – unlike in the 1960s and '70s – intimate life, including sexual relationships, is rarely considered a key battleground. Fighting systems – capitalism, patriarchy, white supremacy – is considered more important political work than changing individual behaviours and lives. This makes sense: changing our lives alone, so far as that is even possible, won't change the world.

Non-normative relationships and sex are not necessarily 'more radical', anyway. Certainly, such intimacies can mirror and recreate the oppressive dynamics common to heterosexuality. Patriarchal domination, for example, can live on in queer couples, or polyamorous triads. 'The tradition of all dead generations weighs like a nightmare on the brains of the living', wrote Karl Marx. 'And just as they seem to be occupied with revolutionising themselves and things, creating something that did not exist before ... they anxiously conjure up the spirits of the past.'[58]

Supposedly 'radical' ways of relating can well be subsumed by capital. As Natasha Lennard writes in her essay 'Policing Desire', 'sexual practices which were once considered threats to capital's reproduction through the family form and property relations' have been eaten up by 'technocapital [that] soothes the status quo: there can be polyamorous configurations with BDSM dungeons in the basement, but the houses are owned'. In the same vein, she asks: 'when there's a popular app for organizing your next queer orgy, how rupturous of our political status quo can the mere fact of such an orgy be?'[59]

But whilst the existence of non-monogamous queers won't topple capitalism, intimate practices do carry political weight:

they *can* be praxis. To deny this can amount to a patriarchal dismissal of the political relevance of the intimate sphere, which is coded as feminine. Experiments in living and relating matter because – amidst everyday and structural violence – they can expand the realm of the possible and prefigure the future.

Today's queer spaces – essential sources of joy, refuge, solidarity and resistance – have their genealogy in sexual dissidence. In eighteenth-century London, when being queer was a crime punishable by death (under the Buggery Act, this meant any sex that wasn't between a married man and wife), there were more gay locales than there are today.[60] In 'molly houses', gay men and people of multiple genders – including sex workers and other members of the criminalised underclass – met to socialise and have sex. Gender expression was fluid, feminine glamour abounded. In exuberant subversion of heterosexual rituals in which sex is obscured, 'Mother Clap', in her molly house in London, facilitated 'marriages', which often included exhibitionist sex, in 'The Marrying Room'. Houses like Mother Clap's were frequently raided, their attendees fined, imprisoned and murdered by the authorities.

Renegade Marxist psychoanalyst Wilhelm Reich argued that the shame-laden repression of sexuality – compelled by 'marriage as a tie, family as a duty, fatherland as a value in itself, morality as authority, religion as an obligation deriving from eternity'[61] – was integral to capitalism's requirement for submissive workers and the reproduction of oppressive ideologies. In his 1933 book, *The Mass Psychology of Fascism*, which the Nazis banned and burned, he theorised that the unleashing of sexual desire and pleasure – undoing 'the ossification of the human plasma' – would be revolutionary.[62]

From the 1960s through to the 1980s, socialist second-wave feminists in the women's liberation movement resisted oppressive sexual orders by organising consciousness-raising projects and attempting to build alternatives to the monogamous heterosexual couple and the nuclear family, which many saw as forces for women's oppression.

The Red Collective in London sought to develop theory about relationships and sex from a materialist perspective by practising sexual relationships that challenged the dyadic form. 'We have tried to change the interconnection between sexual, political and domestic relations', they explain in *The Politics of Sexuality in Capitalism.*[63] Three people in The Red Collective – Anne and Mary, who both had romantic and sexual relationships with Pete and others – documented and analysed their experiences with non-monogamy, linking them to wider political struggles. Decentring the monogamous heterosexual couple as the nucleus of their personal lives and political organising, they found, was generative for their own relationships as well as for their group's sense of solidarity and political work: 'As there was no set way of behaving or conducting relationships for us to fall into, we had to work out everything and construct the principles, and this meant working out what we wanted to do in being together, rather than just establishing a modus vivendi*.'[64]

Is the modus vivendi of straightness doomed? 'Heteropessimism' (later termed 'heterofatalism') was coined by the writer Asa Seresin to refer to a sentiment among people – usually cis women – that considers being straight an affliction. For the heteropessimist, being straight means being condemned to relate closely and sexually with men under patriarchy – with all the violence, unequal power, laborious drudgery, boredom and frustration that will likely entail. It was for this reason that some straight women in the feminist second wave practised and advocated for 'political lesbianism'. Seresin, however, argues that straight women's 'performative distancing' from

---

* Meaning 'a way of life'.

heterosexuality 'is usually little more than an abdication of responsibility'. They conclude that whilst 'universal queerness and the abolition of gender may be the horizon toward which we are eventually moving', we can't give up on heterosexuality in the meanwhile – 'because tens of thousands of women are currently dying of it every year'.[65] And in the same way that decrying heterosexuality per se won't change its brokenness, 'performative distancing' from its institutions – in compulsory monogamy, marriage and the nuclear family – won't lead to their transformation or abolition.

'Queering' things has become memeified. On Twitter at least, the word has become a joke, because vapid use and over-use often render it meaningless. For example, with reference to the Royal Air Force's appropriation of the Pride flag, the journalist Ben Smoke tweeted: 'queering mass murder #gayboss #loveislove #bombwithpride'. 'To queer' something often equates to a shallow, aesthetic subversion of heterosexual norms, or to 'pinkwashing', in which conservative and capitalist institutions such as corporations, police forces or nation states invoke 'queerness' to mask harmful practices or to gain legitimacy.

The 'normalisation' of queer relationships does not signal the world's transformation away from domination and violence. As Berlant writes, 'LGBTQ couples' becoming 'an ordinary event in the everyday, does not mean that heteronormativity has been vanquished. It might mean that one of its qualities – the couple or the family form, for example – is ruling the moral, legal, economic, and/or social roost in such a way that other-oriented practices might be held in contempt and/or illegalized.'[66] Indeed, increasing 'homonormativity' – a politics and culture that accepts *some* queer people as 'born this way', so long as they subscribe to the norms and institutions of heterosexuality – means that some queer people can exist more freely and safely than others. For example, society is more likely to validate married cis gay men than trans people in non-traditional relationships.

It is not solely the *what* of intimacy that holds its radical potential, but the *why and how*. If attempts at feminist and queer forms of relating no longer pose a threat, how can we make sexual politics a threat again? In asking this question we might honour and learn from, as Rich writes, 'the history of women who – as witches, femmes seules, marriage resisters, spinsters, autonomous widows, and/or lesbians – have managed on varying levels not to collaborate' with patriarchal relationships. Such women, she writes, in all cultures and throughout history, have practised resistance – as far as was made possible by their material circumstances – 'even though attacks against unmarried women have ranged from aspersion and mockery to deliberate gynocide, including the burning and torturing of millions of widows and spinsters during the witch persecutions of the fifteenth, sixteenth, and seventeenth centuries in Europe'.[67] The women Rich lists – those who 'have managed on varying levels not to collaborate' – whilst not all LGBTQIA+, are, according to many definitions, queer.

In *Toward the Queerest Insurrection*, Mary Nardini Gang writes:

Queer is not merely another identity that can be tacked onto a list of neat social categories, nor the quantitative sum of our identities. Rather, it is the qualitative position of opposition to presentations of stability – an identity that problematizes the manageable limits of identity. Queer is a territory of tension, defined against the dominant narrative of white hetero monogamous patriarchy, but also by an affinity with all who are marginalized, otherized and oppressed. Queer is the abnormal, the strange, the dangerous. Queer involves our sexuality and our gender, but so much more. It is our desire and fantasies and more still.

Queer is the cohesion of everything in conflict with the heterosexual capitalist world. Queer is a total rejection of the regime of the Normal.[68]

The gender studies professor Mel Chen, too, considers queerness to be not so much about 'sexual contact among subjects' as about 'social and cultural formations of "improper affiliation", so that queerness might well describe an array of subjectivities, intimacies, beings, and spaces located outside of the heteronormative'.[69]

For Chitty, 'queer' is less an identity or practice, and more about dissent against the state and capital – including 'forms of love and intimacy with a precarious social status outside the institutions of family, property, and couple form'.[70] This, he emphasises, does not mean that apparently 'queer sex' and deviant forms of relating are always inherently revolutionary – indeed, they can even shore up the status quo – but that they have been and can be, depending on who is involved, and at which time in history.

In the senses described above, ideas and practices in romantic relationships and sex might meaningfully be considered 'radical' if they in some way disrupt hegemonic, oppressive forms of social relations, and theorise and create alternatives.

Personal and interpersonal ways of being may form part of this: cultivating creativity and pleasure in a world that would have us submit and suffer can be a form of resistance. For Lorde, in her essay 'Uses of the Erotic: The Erotic as Power', the release and sharing of joy and fulfilment – that 'does not have to be called marriage, nor god, nor an afterlife'[71] – not only in sex, but in harnessing deep feeling in every area of our lives, holds political potential:

when we begin to live from within outward, in touch with the power of the erotic within ourselves, and allowing that power to inform and illuminate our actions upon the world around us, then we begin to be responsible to ourselves in the deepest sense. For as we begin to recognize our deepest feelings, we begin to give up, of necessity, being satisfied with suffering and self-negation, and with the numbness which so often seems like their only alternative in our society. Our acts against oppression become integral with self, motivated and empowered from within ... Recognizing the power of the erotic within our lives can give us the energy to pursue genuine change within our world, rather than merely settling for a shift of characters in the same weary drama. For not only do we touch our most profoundly creative source, but we do that which is female and self-affirming in the face of a racist, patriarchal, and anti-erotic society.[72]

Intimate experiences and commitments can fuel us to survive and fight forces of domination – and more consciousness about the ways we relate could open us up to more liberatory relationships, with more authentic communication, consent and connection.

The *Make Your Own Relationship User Guide* zine by relationship and sex educators and writers Meg-John Barker and Justin Hancock aims to support people to 'try a more consensual and intentional way of doing relationships'.[73] The authors consider how reductive our culture of love is, inviting readers to reflect upon, for example, the Ancient Greeks' seven kinds of love, and where their relationships might fit into those. The zine creates opportunities for people to think through their desires and needs, including around communication, interdependence, transparency and the 'relationship escalator'.* Rather than assuming a normative romantic relationship style, it explores a wide variety of options, including monogamy, 'monogamish', open relationships, swinging and solo polyamory.

Reflecting on our personal relationships may throw limiting assumptions – often with their roots in oppressive frameworks – into question. But this doesn't necessarily mean our preferences or choices will change. In examining our desires in terms of the 'relationship escalator', for instance, we might realise the problems with, and want to challenge, the dominance of this script – and decide we want that kind of life regardless. Rethinking our relationships is not about inverting the existing moral order, replacing it with a new 'radical' order. Whatever our choices, being conscious of why we are making them could allow for more intentional, connected and free relationships – which might support us to participate more fully in the struggles of the world around us.

One relationship style referenced in the *Make Your Own Relationship User Guide* is 'relationship anarchy' (RA). Coined in 2006 by Swedish feminist and computer scientist Andie Nordgren,[74] RA proposes that how we construct, conduct and prioritise our relationships should be a creative endeavour. The philosophy is not one in which 'anything goes' – as is often wrongly inferred from 'anarchy' – but one that advocates for bespoke commitments: collaborative relationships built around the people involved, as opposed to 'common sense' approaches and hierarchies. It seeks to remedy the fact that, as hooks asserts, 'a culture of domination [has raised the] … romantic relationship up as the single most important bond, when of course the single most important bond is that

---

* Coined by Amy Gahran in 2012 to describe the series of escalating milestones romantic relationships are expected to meet by heteronormativity – from dating and sexual exclusivity, to marriage and kids.

of community'.[75] This hierarchy is not inevitable, she argues, pointing out that marriage has often been conceived as part of, not apart from, communal life.

Relationship anarchy means that traditional coupledom is not automatically deemed more important than other kinds of relationships. For some, relationship anarchy might simply mean looking afresh at a long, monogamous marriage and deciding that life would be richer if friendships received a similar amount of care and attention; or it might mean realising that a life without 'the One' is just as valuable, and that 'the love of your life' could be your community, or yourself. For others, relationship anarchy might mean inventing relationships entirely from scratch. It could mean deciding to form a domestic partnership with a friend, or freeing a romantic relationship from the traditional, heteronormative markers of 'success' or 'commitment'. It could mean deciding to co-parent with a committed group of friends and having a romantic partnership outside of this – or more than one, or none; or to raise children with a primary romantic partner, living alongside and supported by an intentional community of friends. Like the composition of any one human relationship, the possibilities for human relationships per se, are infinite.

Freedom from normative frameworks is especially important for people who are always already marginalised by dominant discourses around sex and romantic love. In challenging the narrative that sex and romantic love are universal and peak experiences, we have much to learn from asexual and aromantic people. In 'an aromantic manifesto', yingchen and yingtong propose that 'romance is inherently queerphobic' because, in its heteronormative capitalist logic, many queer people are marginalised and excluded as unlovable and undesirable.[76] In proposing 'aromanticism as queer counterpublic', the authors advocate for queer intimacy beyond the competition of romance; for happiness to be freed from romance;

for physical and emotional intimacy beyond the monopoly of romance; for the rejection of marriage as a means of concentrating wealth; for the transformation of queer intimacy into solidarity and political action; and for 'new nonviolent pleasures and desires that do not yet exist'.[77]

In *Life Isn't Binary: On Being Both, Beyond and In-between*, Meg-John Barker and Alex Iantaffi ask: 'What happens to our understandings of love and relationships if we challenge this binary [between romantic partners and friends] and consider treating lovers more like friends and friends more like lovers?'[78] The writers also consider what harms could be avoided and what personal and political possibilities open up if we challenge other relationship binaries: together/single, monogamous/non-monogamous, romantic/sexual and self/other.

Decolonial or anti-colonial thought is instructive around more expansive ways of relating. TallBear considers how one interpretation of sexual monogamy – when adopted as a form of 'compulsory settler sexuality'[79] rather than as a mutual, conscious choice – could be 'hoarding another person's body and desire, which seems at odds with the broader ethic of sharing that undergirds extended kinship'.[80] She posits that her ancestral Indigenous Dakota principle of 'being in good relation-with' could spur more de-objectified, nurturing and just relationships, spanning more widely than the couple form and the nuclear family – indeed, including nonhuman animals and our environments – that might 'fortify me and make me more available to contribute in the world'.[81]

Culturally, romantic and sexual relationships hold existential significance, yet we are still afforded relatively little freedom in this sphere – by the state, by our families, by our selves. The relationships in which we are told we will find much of life's meaning and purpose – whether we do or not – carry weight in how the world is made and remade. Our interdependencies, loving or violent, can percolate upwards, to how we exist in and impact upon the world. 'My love, your love reinforces my fighting instincts. It tells me to go to war', wrote Angela Davis to George Jackson.[82]

The Russian revolutionary and feminist Alexandra Kollontai considered love a political force and proposed 'love-comradeship' to describe the solidarity and political movement-building that is made possible through networks of commitment and care beyond the monogamous marriage and nuclear family, in which care is traditionally siphoned inwards, towards the preservation of the unit. 'Bourgeois morality demanded all for the loved one', she writes. 'The morality of the proletariat demands all for the collective.'[83]

Militant lesbians and gays at the end of the 1960s, including David Fernbach in Britain, suggests ME O'Brien, 'envisioned eros as a potentially liberating source of human freedom' powering their radical political groups fighting for causes including anti-imperialism and socialism: 'It was erotic solidarity, more than any shared essential identity, that would provide the praxis for a gay communism.'[84]

Imagining that our most intimate relationships could exist 'otherwise' might entail new visions for mutual aid, collective care and resource sharing which, in turn, might build bottom-up power. Decentring the couple and the nuclear family form as the loci of quasi-commoning, and cultivating more extensive intimate commitments to, and modes of sharing with, those around us – including nonhuman beings – should better undergird our collective resilience and revolutionary movements.

In shifting our outlook on love, Erich Fromm proposes we make a distinction between 'having mode' and 'being mode'. In societies driven by competition, ownership and greed, he argues, 'having mode' relationships prevail, in which 'each partner seeks the other like a shipwrecked sailor seeks a plank

– for survival'. Fromm argues that such relationships 'are heavy, burdened, filled with conflicts and jealousies', and that this 'having mode' extends upwards, in nations that 'cannot help waging war'.[85] In 'being mode' relationships, on the other hand:

> private having (private property) has little affective importance, because I do not need to own something in order to enjoy it ... Nothing unites people more (without restricting their individuality) than sharing their admiration and love for a person; sharing an idea, a piece of music, a painting, a symbol; sharing in a ritual – and sharing sorrow. The experience of sharing makes and keeps the relation between two individuals alive; it is the basis of all great religious, political, and philosophical movements.[86]

Lovers for liberation

It can be very difficult to build relationships outside of normative frameworks. Even if people experience non-normative desires as an essential aspect of who they are – rather than as a choice – there can be material as well as psychic and social barriers to living them out. 'The personal is not political because personal choices are necessarily political choices', Lennard writes, 'but because the very terrain of what gets to be a choice and what types of persons get to be choosers – what types of persons get to be – are shaped by political power'.[87]

The choice to marry or not, for instance, has not been free, most of all for women, for most of human history. And whilst the pressure to marry is thankfully weaker today for many younger people than it was for older generations, in many cases it remains – at least partially – an unfree 'choice'. Some people are compelled to marry by tradition, culture, family or religion. Marriage may also be a survival mechanism, for example for those who would be unable to obtain visas, access public services or afford to live without a legal spouse. Even for queer people, who may have only accessed the *right* to marry in recent years, the social, economic and financial compulsion to marry or cohabitate as a couple is significant.

In society as it stands, getting married may have irresistible or essential material benefits: for buying a home, for tax relief, for social harmony, for child-rearing, for pooling incomes. In short, in some important ways, being in a marriage or marriage-like relationship might make life easier.

Decolonising love, argues TallBear, is not a simply personal decision, but something that requires us to fight battles against the structures that attempt to pre-empt, coerce and fix the shape of relationships:

> Decolonization is not an individual choice. We must collectively oppose a system of compulsory settler sexuality and family that continues building a nation upon Indigenous genocide and that makes Indigenous and other marginalized relations as deviant. This includes opposing norms and policies that reward normative kinship ties (e.g., monogamous legal marriage, nuclear biological family) over other forms of kinship obligation.[88]

Even the act of sex is to a large extent predetermined by our material realities. Whether someone has access to a safe home, what condition their home is in, who they live with, whether they can afford enough to eat, how much and how hard they work, how sick or exhausted they are, whether they have access to contraceptives and abortion; all these factors influence the possibilities of the erotic. Who gets to experience pleasure is a political question. As the radical queer organisers Queer to the Left demanded in 1990s–2000s United States: 'Everyone deserves a place to fuck. Affordable Housing NOW.'[89]

This extends to the kinds of intimate relationships that feel – or are – possible. A common retort to polyamory, for example, is: 'Who has time for that?! I barely have time for one partner!' Indeed: who does? In life and love as we currently know them, sustaining more than one committed partnership might well feel difficult or impossible – whether logistically, materially or emotionally – especially for those with less resources. As the author and educator Kevin A. Patterson writes in his book about race and polyamory, *Love's Not Color Blind*: 'So, when do you engage in all that valuable relationship-affirming communication? In the limited space between your full-time, minimum-wage shift, and your part-time, minimum-wage shift? Do you find time on the phone, while taking public transportation to pick your children up from school or daycare? Do you find the time after you get home from washing dishes ... but before you have to write a paper for one class and study for an exam in the other?'[90]

Most people struggle under capitalism to locate enough time and energy to nurture relationships at all. Being able to tend to our intimate relationships should not be a privilege. It is a devastating reality that so much of our lifeforce is directed towards labour, rather than love. While 'Who has time for that?' is often a throwaway dismissal of the idea that people might maintain more than one intimate partnership, it could instead be a question of intimate justice. Rather than giving up on alternative visions for our relationships as inexorably impossible, and rather than cajoling individuals to build 'radical' relationships that may not make sense for their lives, let us imagine and fight for a future in which multitudinous love, in multivalent forms, will be conceivable for everyone.

Some of this political work must come from within the intimate realm itself, as it always has. The Wages for Housework campaign – launched by the International Feminist Collective in 1972 – demanded that women's labour in marriage and the nuclear household under capitalism be cate-gorised as work, and therefore its refusal as strike. 'They say it is love. We say it is unwaged work. They call it frigidity. We call it absenteeism', proclaimed Federici's *Wages against Housework*, explaining: 'We want to call work what is work so that eventually we might rediscover what is love and create what will be our sexuality which we have never known.'[91] To this day, such resistance is invoked in calls – for example, by the actor Bette Midler in response to the 2021 anti-abortion law in Texas – for women to mount (heterosexual) sex strikes as a form of protest. Structural power overwhelmingly shapes the intimate realm; but the intimate realm must also organise to challenge structural power.

Whatever 'radical' romance and sex might be, it is not simply about choices and behaviours. The possibility of meaningful agency in this sphere will not come from the proliferation of polyamorous life coaches advertising their services on Instagram, nor from the representation of 'queer families' or 'chosen families' in mainstream advertising cam-paigns. Liberation requires structural change – from secure housing for all, to freedom from exploitation at work, to free childcare. 'Radical' sex and relationships won't topple capital-ism, but toppling capitalism might just make them possible. In the meantime, no matter what kinds of relationships we are in, trying earnestly to be loving – and not to treat each other like commodities – would be a good start.

CHAPTER THREE

They're all you've got

If it is easier to imagine the end of the world than the end of capitalism, it is still perhaps easier to imagine the end of capitalism than the end of the family.

Sophie Lewis

Your children are not your children
They are the sons and daughters of Life's longing for itself.
They come through you but not from you,
And though they are with you yet they belong not to you.

Kahlil Gibran

'Britney knows that her daddy loves her', Vivian L. Thoreen, the lawyer for Spears' father, told the US publication *People* in March 2021, months prior to his suspension from her conservatorship.[1] Britney, meanwhile, says that her family has lived off her exploitation, leaving her 'traumatised'; that her father 'loved the control, to hurt his own daughter';[2] that he is 'obsessed' with her.[3] 'You're allowing my dad to ruin my life', she pleaded with a judge. 'I have to get rid of my dad.'[4]

In November 2021, a judge ended a conservatorship that had limited her freedom for almost 14 years. During those 14 years, Spears released three albums, appeared on television, and had a residency in Las Vegas. Yet, since a mental health crisis in 2008, when she was detained in psychiatric hospitals twice, she was deemed unfit for autonomy. Under the legal guardianship, her father Jamie Spears and others had strict control over intimate aspects of her life, including decisions about her finances, career, medication, relationships and seeing her children. Court records show the conservatorship dictated everything from the colour of her kitchen cabinets, to who she could see, to her use of the contraceptive coil. According to the documentary *Controlling Britney Spears*, her father – who has been accused of physical and verbal abuse[5] – also placed her under 24-hour surveillance, bugging her home and her phone.

Now that Britney is 'free' – thanks in part to the #FreeBritney campaign that had been, like Spears herself, dismissed as 'crazy' – it is widely known that she was exploited by her father. The profits of her labour as a pop star were tightly controlled by him, and over the years of her conservatorship she was forced to pay him nearly $20,000 per month, as well as cover legal fees and the cost of psychiatric interventions she did not consent to.[6]

Like babies born into capitalism everywhere, to her family, Spears was a sort of property. She was, as Sophie Lewis puts it, a product of the tendency among nuclear families to make 'babies in the shape of personal mascots, psychic crutches, heirs, scapegoats, and fetishes, not forgetting avatars of binary sex'.[7] Now she has been released from her father's authority, Spears herself wants 'the real deal', telling the court she wants to 'get married and have a baby'. Why would someone so harmed by the institution of the family want to make one herself? Why does anyone? Because of an inevitable biological drive? Because it's where love lives? Or something else?

Family and how it fucks us up

The nuclear family – a monogamous couple and their offspring, who reside in a private household – has a short history, with its roots in white supremacist heteropatriarchal capitalism. This way of organising society, into small atomised units, was designed in the service of capital, and yet it has been naturalised, ahistoricised and generally accepted as a politically neutral, universal moral good. The Universal Declaration of Human Rights itself states that: 'The family is the natural and fundamental group unit of society and is entitled to protection by society and the State.'

In *The Communist Manifesto*, Karl Marx and Friedrich Engels wrote: 'The bourgeoisie has torn away from the family its sentimental veil, and has reduced the family relation to a mere money relation.'[8] With the growth of industrial capitalism, the dominant kinship structure in the West came to be the nuclear family: a heterosexual marriage with a male breadwinner, and children raised in a private household. This form replaced earlier, more diverse household arrangements, including more collective forms of living with extended families or non-biological kin. As a social unit, the nuclear family imposed sexual monogamy on women because of anxieties about keeping inheritance within the patriarchal bloodline. Marriage did not come with the expectation of sexual exclusivity for men until much more recently.

Besides hoarding property and wealth, the family serves other functions for capital. Rather than placing demands on the state or communal support networks, the family privatises care. In the unpaid drudgery of women, domestic labour is social reproduction: cooking, cleaning and other life-sustaining support that keeps workers alive enough to work, and babies alive enough to grow up to be workers themselves.

The family, too, functions as – to quote the psychoanalyst David Cooper – 'an ideological conditioning device'.[9] The family trains people to perform roles – wife, husband, son, daughter – as befits capitalism, and teaches them the ideologies, including of race, gender and sexuality, upon which the system depends. The benefits of citizenship in many cases are tied to one's membership of a nuclear family.

Whilst the nuclear family was once the reserve of the bourgeoisie, the rise of the workers' movement by the end of the nineteenth century saw it become a symbol of respectability, as ME O'Brien explains:

> The characteristic family ideal of the workers' movement was the single male wage earner, supporting an unwaged housewife, their children enrolled in school, their home a respectable centre of moral and sexual conformity ... This family form was a tremendous victory in improving the standard of living and survival of millions of working-class people, and creating a basis for stable neighbourhood organization, sustained socialist struggle and major political victories. It was also the means by which the workers' movement would distinguish itself from the lumpenproletariat, black workers, and queers. This family form would provide a sexual and gender basis for white American identity and middle-class property ownership.[10]

O'Brien argues that the nuclear family form became a manner by which white people – apart from the poorest and most marginalised like sex workers and queers – set themselves apart from, and cast themselves as superior to, colonised subjects. When Western nations invaded countries in the Global South, enforcing imperialist rule, the institution of marriage and the nuclear family were forced upon colonised people, often replacing more expansive, communal and less patriarchal forms of kinship. Indigenous people, explains Kim TallBear, have endured 'colonial violence against our kin systems', including the 'kidnapping of children of previous generations from Indigenous families who were impoverished by colonialism, and deemed unfit for not attaining the middle-class, nuclear family structures of white colonialists'.[11]

The troubling history of the nuclear family form, of course, does not change the fact that most of us are born into something like it today. Indeed, whilst we may understand its origins in domination and violence, the fact is that many of us depend upon a version of the family as we know it for our survival, and possibly aspire to have 'one of our own someday' (even, or perhaps especially, if our original 'own' was traumatising).

Whilst systemically speaking it has nefarious aims, 'family' as a personal life experience promises to – and sometimes actually does, albeit possibly due to a lack of other options – meet a lot of our needs as humans. Not only is our family supposed to feed us and provide shelter, it is also supposed to nurture our souls, as the foundation of our security, comfort and belonging in the world. For better or worse, the family might be our primary source of care, the place where we get our first lessons in love. And for some, a family might provide refuge from the oppressions of society at large: from the racist state and racism on the streets, from exploitative bosses and heartless work.

Playing happy families

An idealised vision of the family is drilled into us from childhood. At school, from a young age, the family – almost always via heteronormative rhetoric and imagery – is construed as the inevitable, happy and moral culmination of human endeavour. Even if we go home to miserable, disturbing or violent families, at school we draw happy families under bright suns, and rehearse their lives at breaktime. Television, films and advertisements tell us what family should be: ideally, blissful – and if not, at least loyal.

Children, if silently, might be savvy to the dishonesty of this fable. This perhaps explains why children's authors who explore the messy realities of families are so popular. When I was a child, lots of us enjoyed reading Jacqueline Wilson, who was Children's Laureate from 2005 to 2007. Her books depict families struggling with poverty, abuse, homelessness, divorce and unwanted pregnancies. Having grown up in a working-class family, with parents in a rocky relationship, Wilson says that as a child she was troubled by 1950s and '60s books and television, which portrayed 'a soft, pastel world without any serious quarrels or money worries'.[12] She knew 'there was a darker world around'. More recently, now in her 70s, and having ended her four-decades-long marriage to a man and partnered with a woman, she has published a queer love story for teens.

'Family' doesn't keep its promises. Whilst purporting to be a bastion of safety and care, the family as we know it is society's primary breeding ground for the oppression of women and children, gendered violence, queerphobia and transphobia. Government statistics show that of all the women murdered in the year ending March 2020, almost half were killed in their own homes, most likely by a current or former partner or another male family member.[13] This compares to 7 per cent of men killed at home, and 2 per cent by a current or former partner. Referencing the murderousness of the nuclear family for women is but one – extreme – measure of its frequent failure to live up to its 'soft, pastel' ideal. The nuclear family is also where many children are emotionally, physically and sexually abused. It is the social unit in which queer and trans children face their first invalidations, bullying, denials of healthcare and often total rejection. It is where many disabled people have their first experiences of isolation, dearth of care, and ableist abuse.

Reproduction in the nuclear family equates to, as the revolutionary feminist writer Shulamith Firestone put it: 'a-baby-all-your-own-to-fuck-up-as-you-please'.[14] Not only does the nuclear family usually fail to meet its own apparent purpose as a safe and loving haven, it is often the antithesis – the source of our deepest suffering, and concurrently a site of suppression, where trauma is silenced, papered over or denied. Many radical psychoanalysts in the 1960s and '70s, including R. D. Laing, identified the family as having manufactured psychosis in their patients. By inflicting rigid social catego- ries and dynamics, they contended, family structures create untenable internal conflicts that cause what is then understood as 'mental illness'.

The experience of the family as an unsafe arrangement is common, yet scarcely given voice to. Since 'privacy' is a fun- damental building block of the nuclear unit, abuses within it are usually configured as 'private matters', which enables their perpetuation. Just before he was elected as prime minister, Boris Johnson's neighbours called the police on him, having heard his partner Carrie Symonds screaming and shouting 'get off me'. When asked about the incident, Johnson said 'I do not talk about stuff involving my family.'[15]

The state of the family, the state and the family

The modern family looks different to how it did even 50 years ago – some people claim it is now 'broken' or 'under threat'. Certainly, rising divorce rates, 'blended families', single-par- ent households, gay marriage and more women (not only the very richest) outsourcing their domestic labour to poorer women, have changed the shape of the nuclear family – but these factors have not, as some on the right claim, entirely destroyed it as an institution. Among those on the left, anxiety around the apparent demise of the family is more often artic- ulated in assertions that the instability of neoliberal life – with declining wages, precarious work and poor public services – is making 'family life' impossible. They claim that the gov- ernment is not doing enough to ensure people have sufficient money and resources to 'start a family', or is not 'looking after families' in their policies. But it is not only 'families' the state is neglecting; the state is neglecting *people*. It is not doing enough to ensure that *people* – whatever configuration with others (or not) they are living in or want to live in – survive, let alone live fulfilling lives.

It is true that more families today look different from the traditional nuclear form, and it is true that people, including families, are left to languish by the state – but the family as an institution, and the ideologies that underpin it, remains powerful. In 2016, Mark Fisher explained to his students that even though the nuclear family is 'historically, very new', it has assumed 'this quasi-transcendental normativity'.[16] He asked them if anyone had lived in a commune, to no response, and lamented that as little as 20 years ago, there probably would have been some people in the room who had. As he saw it, young people were increasingly resigned to the nuclear family form – compared, say, to when he was at school in the 1980s, when 'there were fairly serious debates about alternatives'.[17] This fact was a 'tragedy', he felt, especially because the idealisation of family doesn't reflect most people's experience of it at all. Family today, he said, might be 'empirically weak but it's transcendentally strong'.[18]

In many respects, the neoconservatism that arose in the 1960s, to push back against the liberation movements and their challenge to the dominance of the nuclear family, is burgeoning today. Threats to rights related to gender and sexuality are gaining force. The 'family values' agenda – which advocates for the preservation and propagation of the institution of the traditional nuclear family as a matter of morality – is gaining strength. This agenda has its modern origins in far-right evangelism in the United States, where conservative Christian groups campaign against abortion, divorce, queer relationships and sex outside of marriage. And they are influential: in 2022, abortion bans swept the US.

These groups actively seek to further their cause in Europe. The US-based International Organisation for the Family, a network of pro-family, anti-feminist, queerphobic religious leaders and politicians, holds the World Congress of Families, a designated hate group.* In 2017, the journalist Claire Provost attended the summit in Budapest, Hungary, undercover. She wrote of the event:

> The conference programme described its goal as 'to unite and equip leaders to promote the natural family'. Speakers were explicit: this means a married mother and father and their children. They name-checked diverse fights against comprehensive sexuality education, abortion, same-sex marriage, 'gender ideology', surrogacy, and euthanasia. But they called for positive, 'winning messages', alliances, and strategies that go after 'hearts and minds' – recalling the shorthand used repeatedly by the US for winning over supporters and public opinion in the context of wars. Several speakers talked specifically about 'appropriating the language' of human rights to bolster conservative campaigns … The theme of the summit – 'Building Family-Friendly Nations: Making Families Great Again'.[19]

But whilst it is growing in new ways, the pro-nuclear-family agenda has long been sturdy on our shores. In 1987, Margaret Thatcher told *Women's Own* magazine that people had grown too dependent on the government for support.[20] She said that people were 'casting their problems on society' but that 'there is no such thing'. Rather, she insisted, 'There are individual men and women and there are families.'

---

* By the extremism-monitoring group Southern Poverty Law Centre.

During his leadership, David Cameron became very concerned with 'broken Britain', blaming 'troubled families' and the 'slow-motion moral collapse' of the country. To whip families into shape, he announced a 'social and security fightback', which included riot training for thousands more police officers.[21] This ideology, of 'the broken family breaking Britain', was reinforced in popular culture – for example when Anne Robinson, the presenter of the gameshow *The Weakest Link*, bullied a single mother of three children for receiving state benefits. She also asked her, 'What happened to the husband?', if she had 'gone gay', and whether her children had 'tags on their ankles'.[22]

Cultural discourse and government policy pursue the model of two parents bringing up children in a private household, requiring as little as possible from their community and the state. The nuclear family is upheld by the state, which, as the sociologist Melinda Cooper writes in *Family Values: Between Neoliberalism and the New Social Conservatism*, is 'willing to enforce – indeed create – legal relationships of familial obligation and dependence where none have been established by mutual consent'.[23] In the United States, she points out, this meant welfare was restructured during the New Deal specifically to subsidise (white) normative lifestyles: Black single or unmarried mothers could not claim benefits.

Today, it would be a mistake, argues Cooper, 'to think that neoliberalism is any less invested in the value of the family than are social conservatives'.[24] Via multifarious policy measures, governments incentivise the traditional nuclear family, contributing to the pre-constitution of desire. Former prime minister Boris Johnson – who has been divorced twice and has conceived seven children with three mothers, including one during an extramarital relationship – reigned over policy that promotes a traditional family set-up. As neoliberal economic policy divests from healthcare, education and benefits, the nuclear family is presumed to replace state support. Marriage is incentivised – now, too, for people in gay partnerships – and inheritance and next-of-kin legal frameworks make bloodline relationships advantageous in scenarios such as death, rendering non-marital, non-biological bonds largely irrelevant.

Marriage certificates and genetic relationships carry weight in immigration and asylum processes. Married straight couples – if they can prove the relationship is not a 'sham' – have a better chance of being granted visas under 'family reunion'; for queer and unmarried partners, being granted residency is much more difficult, often impossible. For all partnerships, consideration for reunion across borders requires certain criteria to be met, for the relationships to count as 'genuine'. For instance, Home Office guidance states that couples must have cohabited 'in a relationship akin to marriage' for a minimum of two years and intend 'to live together permanently'.[25] Having children together and sharing finances is further evidence of a 'genuine' relationship. Biometric data is collected to confirm people's identities and to determine their 'real' family.

In reality, border violence tears families – even 'real' families – apart. Family separation is barbaric – the UK is the only country in the EU that refuses child refugees the right to be reunited with their parents or siblings. In critiques of such border violence, what is rarely acknowledged is the fact that people have other attachments – non-biological and non-legally certified – that matter deeply, perhaps more. In ignoring this fact, we naturalise the moral superiority of normative understandings of family. 'Keep families together' may be an expedient slogan when campaigning for humane immigration laws but, as Lewis notes, for some people – especially queers, who are much more likely to be fleeing their family of origin, and to be yearning for other kinds of kin – the slogan 'is a literally homicidal notion'.[26]

Loyalty to the historically recent custom of splitting off into small family units is not the reserve of the right. Recent years have seen the rise of what is sometimes called the 'trad left'. In 2021, Labour leader Keir Starmer rebranded his platform with a socially conservative and boring 12,000-word essay for the Fabian Society, in which he avoided mentioning socialism and advocated for 'hard-working families'.[27] The essay mentions 'family' 21 times and concludes with ten proposals for a 'contribution society', the first being: 'We will always put hard-working families and their priorities first.'[28] But, he hastens to add, his are 'not conservative or backwards ideas'.[29] In contrast, his predecessor Jeremy Corbyn planned to remove the marriage tax allowance, a financial benefit for those with a legal spouse.

As recently as the 1970s, the abolition of the nuclear family was a reasonably common and well-understood demand among revolutionaries. Family abolitionism contends that the institution of the nuclear family is not only an oppressive and often violent kinship ideal, but also a profoundly inadequate one, in terms of the connection, love and care we require and desire to live well in the world. Family abolitionists propose alternative visions for kinship that might better nourish us, communalising the care work that is currently privatised.

Having been mostly killed off in the 1980s – when feminism opted for a reformist approach to the family instead – family abolitionism and utopian thought are seeing a revival. This trajectory reflects the growing force of abolitionist politics in general on the left. The 2020 global rising of the Black Lives Matter[*] movement, in response to the murder of George Floyd by a white police officer, ignited and strengthened calls for police abolition. Movements to abolish other oppressive

---

[*] Founded in 2013 after Trayvon Martin's murderer was acquitted.

institutions have also gained strength, for example around psychiatry and education.

The demand for 'family abolition' is often met with dismay or ridicule. Sometimes this is because people imagine family abolitionists want to bulldozer their family in particular, or to belittle their personal desire for solace within a traditional family unit. These are not the goals of family abolitionism; family abolition does not want to kill your husband or make you hate your parents. Instead, it asks for the flourishing of all the things that the nuclear family promises but does not deliver: cradling kinship for everyone, characterised by loving commitment, safety, care and camaraderie. Looking at the evidence, family abolition is conscious that the family as we know it is failing us, and that we need to create new ways to look after each other, beyond blood.

Nevertheless, calling for the upheaval of social mores is always, in the end, going to provoke moral panic in some – especially those whom the current conventions are better serving. In December 2021, there was a 'normie shitstorm'* about family abolition on Twitter, with someone asserting that it was an idea pursued by 'asocial weirdos' and 'very odd people obsessed with mad and bizarre minoritarian rubbish'.[30]

In fact, the radical critique of the family has a long and rich history, attached to Black feminism. As the writer and researcher Lola Olufemi tweeted in response to leftists' reactivity around family abolition: 'read one black woman on kinship pls ... You're crying over whether or not Engels said it when it's been focal to black studies/black feminism for decades.'[31] Family abolition today is often informed by a 1987 article by literary critic and Black feminist scholar Hortense J. Spillers entitled 'Mama's Baby, Papa's Maybe', which argues

---

* As dubbed by Richard Seymour: https://salvage.zone/abolition-notes-on-a-normie-shitstorm

that the nuclear family is fundamentally shaped by white supremacy, and is part of an apparatus of power through which Black women in the United States are gendered differently to white women. In her analysis, Black families – as with queer and poor families – have not been truly accepted by the dominant culture as 'families' at all: '"Family", as we practise and understand it "in the West" – the vertical transfer of a bloodline, of a patronymic, of titles and entitlements, of real estate and the prerogatives of "cold cash", from *fathers to sons* and in the supposedly free exchange of affectional ties between a male and a female of his choice – becomes the mythically revered privilege of a free and freed community.'[32] However, she writes, 'African peoples in the historic Diaspora had nothing to prove, *if* the point had been that they were not capable of "family" (read "civilization"), since it is stunningly evident ... that Africans were not only capable of the concept and the practice of "family", including "slaves," but in modes of elaboration and naming that were at least as complex as those of the "nuclear family" "in the West."'[33]

Today, the BLM movement has challenged the nuclear family, stating: 'We disrupt the Western-prescribed nuclear family structure requirement by supporting each other as extended families and "villages" that collectively care for one another, especially our children, to the degree that mothers, parents, and children are comfortable. We foster a queer-affirming network. When we gather, we do so with the intention of freeing ourselves from the tight grip of heteronormative thinking.'[34] The rest of the statement, on a page of the site that has now been removed, clarifies that BLM is committed to 'family' in other senses – in supporting parents and in affirming 'the global Black family'.

As the writer Jude in London argued in response to the 'asocial weirdos' tweet, critiques of the family 'are not bourgeois or elitist concepts that "normies" cannot understand.

Most working-class people understand it perfectly well because, globally, most working-class people are already doing it. They are already raising children that aren't theirs with friends, siblings, cousins, partners, neighbours. Because it is all they've ever known culturally. Abolish The Family is a call to normalise this, not to take your granny away.'[35] Indeed, family abolitionist principles aren't nearly as dramatic as some detractors fear. Cuba's new legal definition of the family, for example, is as simple as it is radical: 'a union of people linked by an affective, psychological and sentimental bond, who commit themselves to sharing life such that they support each other'.

Now is an apposite moment for the revival of family abolitionism. The pandemic and the ecological crisis it was born from might seem to some like good reasons to drill down into bourgeois, insular family units, to hoard resources and direct survival instincts towards genetic futurity. But, as the pandemic has exposed, the nuclear family is a devastatingly inadequate support group – one that, on its own, will not keep all of us alive. If we rely upon it as our main provision for kinship and care, even more so as we descend into further social catastrophe, marginalised people will continue to face increasing exclusion, neglect, violence and death.

Remaking the world by remaking the family does not mean throwing the baby out with the bathwater. Amidst the violence of the nuclear family, there are ideas and values we might salvage from the wreckage. Presently, the family is experienced as a dependable source of love, care and safety only by the fortunate few – we must demand this experience *for all*.

A 'positive supersession of the family', argues O'Brien, means:

> the preservation and emancipation of the genuine love and care proletarian people have found with each other in the

midst of hardship: the fun and joy of eroticism; the intimacy of parenting and romance. This love and care, transformed and generalized, is what is to be preserved in the abolition of familial domination. Loosened from the rigid social roles of heteronormative gender and sexual identity, the material constraints of capitalism, and remade in the intensity of revolutionary struggle, the potential of love and care can be finally freed onto the world. The abolition of the family must be the positive creation of a society of generalized human care and queer love.[36]

Loyalty and forgiveness are two more 'family values' worth examining as we imagine and create kinship beyond the nuclear and biological. Whilst, at one end of the spectrum, families frequently reject queer offspring out of hand, at the other, they purport to be bastions of support 'through thick and thin'. What this often looks like in practice is brushing harm under the carpet. Because 'family comes first', because 'we're still family at the end of the day', neglect, abuse and violence are often permitted within its ambit. The loyalty and forgiveness families sometimes show *some* members usually looks nothing like transformative justice; accountability is rare in cultures of domination and silence. Nevertheless, there may be a helpful granule, at least, in the nuclear family's false claim to unshakable devotion: the idea that no one is disposable.

In an abolitionist future, a care commune cannot be carceral; it cannot respond to harm with further harm through punishment and ejection. When people hurt each other – as all of us do – we must not turn away, but stand by the person who has been harmed and be led by their needs, whilst supporting the perpetrator to take responsibility, make efforts to repair, and change their behaviour.

The idea is that family is 'bound by blood'. And whilst this principle is responsible for much agony, people who make biological babies often claim that from having progeny there springs hope. Having reproduced, parents recount discovering a new fervour for the future, or being instilled with a greater sense of stewardship over the planet. Could some sense of parental futurity extend outwards, beyond the genetic, to help give birth to a better world? If children are the future, how might making children differently reshape the future? Or, as the activist and scholar Loretta J. Ross asks: 'How do we get from a conservative definition of mothering as a biological destiny to mothering as a liberating practice that can thwart runaway capitalism?'[37]

In *Revolutionary Mothering: Love on the Front Lines*, independent scholar and activist Alexis Pauline Gumbs writes about mothering – 'especially the mothering of children in oppressed groups, and especially mothering to end war, to end capitalism, to end homophobia and to end patriarchy' – as 'a queer thing'.[38] Mothering might be a way to recreate the self and the world; or as Gumbs puts it, a way of 'breaking cycles of abuse by deciding what we want to replicate from the past and what we need urgently to transform'.[39]

Resisting the forces of ecological disaster could indeed be spurred on by wanting a bright future for 'your' child; but caring for the planet need not be – must not be – contingent upon having biological offspring. Many Indigenous cultures hold the responsibility of care for all life dear. Ecologies are not simply protected 'so my kids can enjoy them', but for their own sake, and for the sake of all beings. In this understanding, ecologies are not protected so that extraction can continue for our kin, but because the land, the air, the water – they *are* our kin. As the author and professor Joseph M. Pierce writes, the practice of 'land acknowledgements' – statements recognising the stewardship of Indigenous peoples over a certain territory – is not enough, because land requires a reciprocal *relationship* of care, not simply confirmation that it exists. What is crucial, he argues, 'is territory as kin, building relationships with that land itself, as if it were your kin. Because it is.'[40] When resisting tar sands pipelines in Minnesota, Indigenous water protectors have carried banners saying 'land defense is a family value'.[41]

Conception can be reimagined beyond baby-making. Together, we can conceive better futures. As Lewis writes:

> Everywhere about me, I can see beautiful militants hell-bent on regeneration, not self-replication. Recognizing our inextricably surrogated contamination with and by everybody else (and everybody else's babies) will not so much 'smash' the nuclear family as make it unthinkable. And that's what needs to happen if we are serious about reproductive justice, which is to say, serious about revolution.[42]

We know it takes a village

The idea that nurturing children takes more than two parents is not radical. We know it takes a village. Even in the most conventional nuclear families, people call upon extended family for support and appoint 'godparents'. The commonplace inadequacy of childcare support networks – especially for those who cannot afford to pay for back-up – has been theorised by Madeline Lane-McKinley and Marija Cetinic as being a cause of 'postpartum depression'. Postpartum depression, they write, 'describes the social conditions of motherhood under late capitalism', which in turn demands 'forms of radical kinship' already visible in 'existing frameworks of solidarity and communality'.[43] Here, Indigenous customs and principles that colonisation attempted to wipe out are instructive. As TallBear argues:

> Perhaps our allegiances and commitments are more strongly conditioned than we realize by a sense of community that exceeds rather than fails to meet the requirements of settler

sex and family. The abuse and neglect in so many Indigenous families born of colonial kidnapping, incarceration, rape, and killing are all too real. But perhaps our relentless moves to caretake in tiospaye[*] more than in normative settler family forms is not simply the best that we can do. Maybe it is the best way to heal?[44]

Even the Scottish government once attempted to formalise a remedy for the nuclear family's scarcity of care, by proposing a 'named person scheme' that would have seen every child in the country being appointed a person external to the family, to keep a check on their well-being. The named person, usually a teacher or health worker, would look out for the child and perform a kind of 'checks and balances' role for the family. The scheme attracted pushback from the Scottish Conservatives as an intrusion on families, and a legal fight against it was led by the Christian Institute, an evangelical lobbying group. As a result, the scheme was mostly scrapped after the Supreme Court found it to be in breach of the right to privacy and a family life under the European Convention on Human Rights. The legal judgment was celebrated by the Christian Institute – which advocates for 'conversion therapy' for queer and trans people – as 'a victory for the freedom of families'.

This 'freedom of families' entails trauma – for, as Paul Jackson writes, when the family is 'closed to the world horrible things can happen'. What would it mean to have 'an open relationship' family, as he puts it?[45] For queers, trans people and other marginalised groups such as sex workers and rough sleepers, mutual, collective mothering in a broader support network has always been the norm. Amongst these communities, kinship networks are chosen and porous – or, as the writer Armistead Maupin has put it, 'logical' family.[46]

---

[*] 'Tiospaye' is a Native American Dakota word referring to extended kinship groups.

While this type of kinship may include communal living, it may also be diffuse, between people who share spaces and moments dedicated to care, connection and community. This could take infinite shapes: shared creative pursuits, childcare cooperatives, support groups, sex parties, festivals, co-authoring, political organising. As the comedian and historian Jules Joanne Gleeson argues: 'for queers, the prospect of putting an end to the domination of private households can come to seem less extreme and more hopeful' because it would mean 'an end to the farce of most queers being raised by heterosexuals'. A communist future, she proposes, relies upon 'the lessons of hustles and community solidarity', as well as the 'prolonged bouts of joy, rarefied skills, and kinds of support that ["fellow exiles" are] uniquely placed to share' being harnessed such that 'the harm done to us by our families is not only mitigated, but actively overcome'.[47]

'Motherhood' (as an exclusionary institution couched in privilege) and 'mothering' (as a practice and an experience) are distinct, argues Adrienne Rich.[48] It follows that anyone can mother – including adults redoing difficult experiences of mothering for each other, and adults caring for children who are not 'their own'. When mothers 'unlearn domination', as Gumbs describes, they might also unlearn possession.[49] She quotes a 1979 edition of the lesbian journal *Off Our Backs*, in which one writer, 'Doc', shares that one of the stated aims of the 'Third World Lesbian and Gay Conference' was that 'All third world lesbians share in the responsibility for the care of nurturing of the children of individual lesbians of color.'[50] In the same journal issue, Mary Peña and Barbara Carey assert that in lesbian families without patriarchal authority, '[CHILDREN] WILL NOT BELONG TO THE PATRIARCHY. THEY WILL NOT BELONG TO US EITHER. THEY WILL BELONG ONLY TO THEMSELVES.'[51]

Black communities have typically practised more collec-tivised approaches to bringing up children, for instance in traditions of informal adoption. As bell hooks charts:

Let's say you didn't have any children and your neighbor had eight kids. You might negotiate with her to adopt a child, who would then come live with you, but there would never be any kind of formal adoption, yet everybody would recognize her as your 'play daughter.' My community was unusual in that gay black men were also able to informally adopt children. And in this case there was a kinship struc-ture in the community where people would go home and visit their folks if they wanted to, stay with them (or what have you), but they would also be able to stay with the person who was loving and parenting them.[52]

Collective child-rearing might also entail communalised domesticity, in place of the private nuclear household. In the 1970s, members of the revolutionary socialist feminist organ-isation Big Flame in England began having children, and questions of child liberation and the gendered division of social reproduction became more pressing within the group. In a 1980 Big Flame discussion bulletin about children and socialism, S.C. writes about her experience of collective child-care in Leeds. The piece opens: 'No section of our society is more under attack in the present crisis than our kids. They are the most vulnerable and powerless of groups and despite Thatcherism's adulatory attitude to the family they are being hammered.' S.C. shares how she and her partner decided to live with another couple in order to resist the 'degree of dependency and possessiveness and insularity' that can come with nuclear family living, and to undermine the institution as part of 'our attempt to undermine the whole system of capi-talist and patriarchal oppression'. The four adults, along with two others living nearby, had babies around the same time, with 'a strong conception of doing it together'. Between them they ran a mini crèche on a rota system of six adults, and on occasion brought other children into the fold.[53]

In this example, collective childcare was part of a wider revolutionary project, which included making political organising accessible for parents and prioritising children's agency. Raising a child confident in the company of those outside their immediate biological family meant that S.C. sometimes felt she didn't 'see enough' of her child. 'But', she writes, 'it is a liberation for her and for me that she actually demands to spend time away. If she is pissed off with me she knows she can take her tea to her friends', get support from others and return when she feels ready.' Prioritising freedom and sociality in this way, they believed, supported radical struggle.

In the context of their political organising, the meaningful inclusion of children as part of the community – rather than isolating them within the domain of the nuclear family – was also a constant reminder to keep things fun and enjoyable wherever possible. S.C. concludes:

> Opening up our relationships with our individual children to others in BF [Big Flame] can be very difficult but it can also be extremely rewarding. In my experience it's the only way to maintain the kind of interest and commitment to the organization that I want. For our kids it can provide an invaluable experience of communism – an experience that can begin to encourage in them the seeds of a creative and positive opposition to the system that oppresses us all.[54]

Between necessity and desire

Today, leftists are more likely to couch their demands in terms of the tragedy of the nuclear family's demise than to call for its abolition. In his essay 'The Road Ahead', Starmer expresses his gratitude that he grew up at a time 'that made it possible for me ... to have a family of my own'.[55] He laments that young people nowadays are more often unable to earn enough money or have sufficiently secure housing to do the same. This is true; it has become much more difficult to – as Starmer puts it – 'put down deep roots'. But 'insecurity and inequality of opportunity' in society do not come down to the viability of the nuclear family. A better future means loving kinship for the many, not the few.

As we build this future, we should keep in mind that 'doing family differently' is not always an active choice people make, but a matter of survival. As O'Brien writes: 'new heterogeneous family structures are a symptom of desperation as much as they are of the practice of care'.[56] Escaping the familiar harm of the family and seeking alternative kinship may well entail enduring different, significant harms elsewhere. The examples O'Brien gives include: 'A queer youth, freed from a violent relationship with their parents, may be subject to the new risks of street-based sex work; young mothers, opting not to marry their abusive boyfriends, may find themselves working long hours in retail service under sexually-harassing managers.'[57] Life outside the nuclear family under capitalism is no utopia; indeed, whilst presenting new possibilities for care, it can be difficult or even perilous.

As the Covid era has taught us, however, finding new ways to care can feel hopeful. Discovering that we cope better with – and find solace and pleasure in – more communal approaches could be prefigurative politics. Everywhere, people were reminded of – or perhaps learned for the first time – the beauty of simply knowing their neighbours. In the growth of mutual aid groups, community-led food co-ops, collaborative home-schooling, and even in the proliferation of whole-street WhatsApp groups (used to coordinate the delivery of provisions to people isolating, or to ask for and offer other kinds of support), there were glimpses of what it might be like to accept that we need each other: more of us, more.

The nuclear family is a scab

A scab in two senses: an injury crusted over by blood, and counter-revolutionary. It offers us what Lauren Berlant describes as 'cruel optimism' – 'when something you desire is actually an obstacle to your flourishing'.[58] 'Normative optimism', argues Berlant, is 'why the exhaustion and corruption of families in the brittle economy produces, nonetheless, a desire in these children for the "normal" life, "the good life"',[59] as with Britney Spears. This is a 'cruel' relation because it promises much and may well end up robbing us of the very things we were seeking, like safety, abundant love, and togetherness.

In what ways is the nuclear family counter-revolutionary, and how could doing things differently, in turn, support revolutionary struggles? The family is a small unit of people, motivated by genetic loyalty, private property and inward-looking priorities. Whilst bio-familial solidarity can be a vital and profound experience, it is generally unconducive to building wider ranging intimacies and comradeship. As Gleeson writes: 'We call for abolishing the family not as a means of disregarding the tireless efforts made by proletarians to preserve the well-being of their relatives, but in awareness that these personal struggles alone will never serve to emancipate us as a class.'[60] Effective political action towards a better world requires us to build meaningful constellations of non-biological kinship, too. As Silvia Federici has said: 'The denuclearisation of the family is the path to the construction of communities of resistance.'[61]

Leanne Betasamosake Simpson explains that the radical resurgent Indigenous struggle against 'dispossession and settler colonialism and the violence of capitalism, heteropatriarchy, white supremacy, and anti-Blackness that maintains them'[62] requires family: 'not the nuclear family that has been normalized in settler society, but big, beautiful, diverse, extended multiracial families of relatives and friends that care very deeply for each other'.[63] Such 'families' demonstrate the symbiotic relationship between intimate life and political action. Indeed, when non-nuclear kinship has been so beleaguered by Empire, as independent scholar carla bergman and the organiser and writer Nick Montgomery argue, it is not a destination, but a political struggle in and of itself: 'Creating intergenerational webs of intimacy and support is a radical act in a world that has privatized child-rearing, housing, subsistence, and decision making.'[64]

Making impossible families possible

Creating and sustaining non-normative families or non-biological kinship groups can be difficult in society as we know it. It could seem impossible. It is made to feel this way, and it will likely remain this way unless we transform the capitalist society that depends upon the nuclear family to function. This could involve resisting government policies that incentivise and privilege particular modes of living. In *The Anti-social Family*, Michèle Barrett and Mary McIntosh argue that feminists and socialists, in the interests of 'greater freedom of choice and the move towards collectivism',[65] must challenge any social policy that strengthens the hegemony of the nuclear family as an institution and makes diverse forms harder. This includes demanding and building a society that does not depend upon the privatised care of the nuclear family, but has the infrastructure to meet everyone's needs for safety and survival without it.

As things stand, non-nuclear kinship can feel precarious, since its survival rests upon the conditions of capitalism, which are particularly hostile to it. Normative modes are encouraged not only by the state, but also by our families of origin and the wider culture – probably even by ourselves, our psyches having developed in this context.

Although it could really be more supportive, kinship beyond the nuclear family is construed as, and often made, untenable for those with children. Author, performer, healer and community worker Kai Cheng Thom writes of her friends' excitement at having babies: 'I used to see my friends' eyes shine that way when we talked about living together, starting a collective, learning how to cultivate food from the land. Growing old together. Dying together.'[66] The problem, as she puts it, is 'that the Revolution never arrived (or, at least, it hasn't yet). The babies, however, did come for us.'[67] These babies, she writes, 'seem to be stealing all of my friends and, with them, my hopes for the future' – because, in capitalist society, raising children isn't a communal thing. It is not that she begrudges her friends' decisions; she wants to be a part of their lives. She even dreams of a conventional lifestyle herself – but as a trans woman, the nuclear family structure does not welcome her: 'Although some might say that growing up means assimilating into heteronormative society, this is not really an option for many queers. It is not an option for me.'[68]

In making non-nuclear kinship possible, we need to look closely at who has more and less autonomy over their bodies and why. In the case of the women's strike movement, this means refusing unwaged and waged social reproduction, and all the work that women do, showing the world that when we stop, the world stops with us.* Transforming society so that more kinds of family open up to us could entail many kinds of strike. Reclaiming our bodies in a society that attempts to have power over them – controlling our access to health-care, including hormones, birth control and abortion – is part of rejecting the oppressions underlying the institution of the nuclear family. In some cases, a strike could mean refusing to reproduce. Lewis explains that for 'gestators of oppressed classes', terminating a pregnancy can be a kind of strike – including when contraceptives and safe abortion have been denied or are not readily accessible. She notes that enslaved women, for instance, 'have used a multitude of tactics to refuse the work of pregnancy and resist participating in the repro-duction of slavery.'[69] Liberating kinship means seizing the means of (re)production in all manner of ways.

Fighting for a broadening of possible alternatives to the nuclear family is also about fighting alongside those who aren't permitted into the ideology in the first place. Because, as bergman and Montgomery argue, 'Challenging the nuclear family is not about puritanical rejection of anything that resembles it; it is about creating alternatives to its hegemony, to the dismembering of social relations.'[70] Increased freedom to build 'families' beyond the nuclear would allow more people to experience enduring group intimacy. It would also allow more people to survive.

Not all happy families are alike

Two Covid Christmases in, more people started looking afresh at what 'family time' means. Some lamented being apart from biological family, perhaps coming to appreciate it anew, being

---

* 'When we stop, the world stops with us' is a common slogan of the current feminist movement internationally.

in the fortunate position that such time spent mostly lives up to its promised gifts of love and togetherness. Others, especially queers, were relieved at the chance to spend the season with chosen family instead, or alone. For everyone, the pandemic has shown that doing family on autopilot is unsustainable.

Despite popular loyalty to the form, it is widely accepted that 'family fucks us up'. Whether through abuse, violence, rejection, neglect or good old-fashioned emotional unavailability, most of us know that the scars family leaves mark us for life. But – though relationships inevitably involve harm – surely our closest kinship bonds should, by and large, be a source of healing. The latter may be found in transforming existing families, or by creating new ones. For some Indigenous populations, TallBear argues, the reclaiming of expansive visions for kinship, which settlers attempted to crush, is itself a path to healing from colonial violence.[71]

Dismantling the hegemony of the nuclear family involves challenging naturalised understandings of social relations. For example – following Meg-John Barker and Alex Iantaffi's suggestion that we might treat 'lovers more like friends and friends more like lovers'[72] – what if we treated non-biological kin more like biological family and biological family more like non-biological kin? This is a question, not a suggestion; there are many ways in which being 'like family to each other' is terrible. At the same time, what if we extended the commitment, care and resource sharing that we primarily understand as the domain of 'family' to other kinds of kin: to friends, to lovers, to nonhuman species, to the land? And what if we brought to our families the same level of communication and boundaries we might try to practise with our friends or lovers? It's the questions that matter.

None of this is easy. And yet, as Barrett and McIntosh remind us: 'If we must avoid the counterproductive stance of self-righteous moralizing, we must also avoid the defeatist

CHAPTER FOUR

A ladder is not a resting place

You can go home again, the General Temporal Theory asserts, so long as you understand that home is a place where you have never been.

Ursula K. Le Guin

Perhaps home is not a place but simply an irrevocable condition.

James Baldwin

The same week our landlord threatened me and my friends with eviction, I went to view a luxury London property. Posing as a rich couple, myself and housing researcher and artist Laura Yuile visited the £3 million townhouse as part of her project Asset Arrest,* 'an estate-agent-agent that handles the process of arranging viewings of properties you have no intention of buying'.[1]

The house we viewed is part of the 12-acre London City Island development in Newham, managed by Bally-more Group – in Laura's estimation, 'among the evilest of the property developers' – in partnership with EcoWorld, a Malaysian developer. The site – not in fact an 'island' at all, but a peninsula of the River Lea – was once known as 'Bog Island' due to its susceptibility to flooding. The develop-

---

* See www.assetarrest.com

ment's foundations have been built using earth dug up for multistorey subterranean extensions in Kensington mansions.

Like many other property developers, Ballymore purports to be engaged in 'regeneration'. That is to say: building expensive flats in poor areas and pricing out established populations – in this case, selling many properties 'off-plan' to non-resident investors.

There is little incentive to design and construct homes to high standards when every corner cut means more money in directors' pockets. Ballymore is also notorious for squeezing every penny of profit possible out of residents in additional charges – including, in one case, charges for renovations after a fire in one of their towers, which the London Fire Brigade said acted like a 'broken chimney' due to a faulty ventilation system.[2] Laura once overheard some site engineers agreeing that, even if they had the money, they would never buy a Ballymore home.

Before viewing the house, Laura and I got into character in the development's 'Homestead' restaurant, eating truffle oil chips and drinking gin and tonics. Then we met our assigned salesperson, who handed us gulp-sized plastic bottles of water with a peroxide grin.

Though the salesperson was probably younger than me – and could also, no doubt, not afford such real estate – I felt childlike being shown around the house. With London home ownership, let alone luxury home ownership, so out of reach, I felt my impersonation of someone for whom it wasn't must have been transparent. I let Laura – experienced at the guise – do most of the talking. 'Is that a walk-in wardrobe?', she asks. 'Yes, it's huge', replies the salesperson, 'the size of most people's studio flats!'

Bookable via a 'concierge app', the development's amenities – the pools, the spa, the gyms, the cinema, the workspace, the art galleries – are open to all and great places to make friends, the salesperson says, assuring us that 'members of the public are not allowed in'. This includes those living in the development's small proportion of 'affordable housing'.

What London City Island is really 'about', says the salesperson – echoing the marketing copy's keywords – is 'close-knit' and 'creative' community. When planning the development, Ballymore contracted Futurecity, 'a global cultural placemaking agency'. The consultants were tasked with building a 'cultural strategy': inventing a simulacrum of artsy neighbourliness to attract buyers. Cultural institutions were lured in: the National Ballet has relocated there, and the developers had been trying to 'get' the London Film School, the salesperson tells us, but they pulled out. Ballymore has also tried to attract small independent artists – some 'quite famous', apparently. When Laura rented an art studio in the development, she was told to tidy it up by site managers, in case the messy creative space, visible through her window, was off-putting for prospective investors.

On the review website Trustpilot.com, Ballymore has mostly 1-star ratings.[*] Residents complain of low-quality, unsafe builds; disrepair; exorbitant and uncapped service charges; and poor communication from the 'monopolistic'[**] company. Senior Ballymore staff have responded to this by drowning out bad reviews with their own 5-star ones, leading Trustpilot to issue a 'cease and desist' letter.[3]

Developers like Ballymore don't intend to sell wellbuilt homes at fair prices; instead, they flog an *idea of home*. In the case of London City Island, this idea amounts to 'an urban warehouse aesthetic' set in 'a hub for creative minds', 'designed to improve wellbeing and socialisation'.[4] Unlike sturdy construction, *concepts* require minimal investment: hire

---

[*] Correct at the time of writing.

[**] Review by 'James' on Trustpilot.com, 17 March 2021.

a 'placemaking' consultant to fabricate an ethos; build a shop-front website to masquerade as an arts blog; print a glossy brochure pretending to be a culture mag; lure in some creative types with impossible-to-refuse rents.

A couple of weeks after our visit, Laura attended a conference for developers held on London City Island called 'Productive Placemaking: New Opportunities – What does successful urban regeneration truly look like?' During the networking time, a developer told Laura's architect persona of his regeneration project: 'We really tried to manufacture a sense of life and in some ways, it paid off.' Another developer, a Ballymore director, confessed: 'Yes, ultimately we have the sinister goal of increasing property prices, but it doesn't mean we don't care about culture!' Newham, where Ballymore built London City Island, is one of London's poorest boroughs. Compared to London averages, the borough has much higher rates of child poverty and homelessness, and the highest rates for evictions and households in temporary accommodation.[5] In recent years, rent in the area has risen twice as fast as wages.[6]

'Home' can mean many things – but, at the very least, feeling 'at home' requires some sense of security. Security in feeling, for instance, that you have a safe place to settle, a place that you can 'make your own', where you won't be forced to leave. In the UK, unless you inherit or can comfortably afford to buy a home, this sense of security is very hard to come by.

'Stay at home' in a housing crisis

Of all the injustices brought home during the Covid-19 pandemic, that of homelessness was stark. When the government was ordering everyone to 'stay at home', as if everyone had one, it became harder for those unaffected to turn away from the experiences of rough sleepers, the houseless, or those in insecure or inadequate housing. Increasing press coverage and grassroots eviction resistance suggested a growing consciousness around the brutality of a housing regime in which landlords are free to throw people out of their homes onto the streets.

In the UK today, the logic of 'home' is configured through the property market, in which people are supposed to invest in 'assets', from which they might extract yet more wealth in the form of rent. In this context, hundreds of thousands of people are homeless, whilst there are over 500,000 homes with no permanent resident. Social housing is shoddy and scarce, and not an option at all for those with no recourse to public funds, including many migrants; private sector rents are extortionate, sucking up a third of most tenants' income, and almost 50 per cent in London; and buying a home is unaffordable for a large proportion of the population due to house prices rising faster than wages. This arid landscape of home – the 'housing crisis' – is the result of decades of government policy favouring wealth accumulation for the few over reliable roofs for everyone. This is no secret to young people: 78 per cent blame capitalism for the housing crisis.[7]

Our homes – though scarcely publicly owned anymore – are part of the architecture of the state. At the start of the 1970s, around a third of homes in Great Britain were affordable local authority housing. Since then, the amount of social housing has declined rapidly. This began in the 1980s, when the right-to-buy scheme, which allowed council tenants to purchase their homes at reduced cost, was accelerated by the Thatcher government in the 1980 Housing Act. New social housing did not keep pace with the declining stock, and the 1988 Housing Act, by empowering housing associations to access private funds to construct and maintain homes, made it even harder for councils to build social housing. Meanwhile, landlordism was made more alluring, as the Act introduced assured shorthold tenancies, contributing to rising house prices.

During the 1980s, mortgages became more accessible, but an increasingly deregulated financial sector meant buyers faced high charges from lenders as well as risky contracts. House prices shot up, before crashing at the end of the decade, with more repossessions forcing more people to give up their homes. In the mid-1990s, house prices started to rise again, as they have done ever since,* and more lenders began offering 'buy-to-let' mortgages: the rental market grew, and buying a home became increasingly unaffordable as price rises far outstripped wage growth. In 2019, the average house price in England was eight times higher than the average yearly earnings of someone working full-time, with this ratio even higher in London.[8] So, since social housing is ever scanter, more people are forced to line the pockets of landlords rather than save for a mortgage that would cost less than their rent.

It was only whilst telling everyone to stay at home during a pandemic that the government was forced introduce measures for (some of) those who couldn't. Overnight – as if conceding that survival being contingent upon having money was an abusive logic – the Tory government banned evictions and ordered local councils to eradicate rough sleeping. Such measures, whilst flawed, proved that rapid societal transformation is possible. But, of course, they were short-lived: landlords were soon as free as ever to turf tenants out at will; additional support for rough sleepers was scrapped. And whilst the state had some tepid offerings for some rough sleepers and renters, many others deprived of homes were left to suffer the physical and mental burdens of the pandemic

---

* Apart from in the years immediately following the 2007 'credit crunch'.

under duress, in institutions such as detention centres, prisons and psychiatric hospitals.

Home is not a haven

The government's 'stay at home' injunction was supposedly simple, except for those for whom it most obviously wasn't. Government announcements were clear: 'stay at home' was invoked as an easy and safe requirement to 'save lives' – such a small ask, of heroic stature. In these invocations, 'home' meant a comfortable place, where we most likely lived along-side our most dear and caring companions. And if not, then a place where they were all just a cup of tea and a video call away: the new paragon of homeliness, as pictured by every other pandemic-era ad.

This domestic mythology is based upon the state's privileged ideology of home – that of the bourgeois nuclear household. According to this way of organising society, everyone should live much of their lives in homes that they own, ideally in a family made up of a married couple with actual or impend-ing offspring. Many people aspire to this vision. Owning a home is seen as an accomplishment – increasingly, a victory 'against the odds'. It has become customary for young people with family money to write articles about 'how I bought my first house at 23', and for couples to post celebratory home-owner photos on social media, dangling their keys like inedible carrots.

The nuclear household is lauded in the media, in advertise-ments, in popular culture and by families (even the mostly unhappy ones) as the best kind of home. But its normativ-ity is likely not the only reason for its popularity. The private family home promises to meet a vital need of which capi-talism deprives us – that of communality. Whilst living in a shared home with friends is only socially acceptable for young

117

adults, living in a family unit could seem to offer a socially celebrated iteration of collective living. Because, Mark Fisher writes, 'living in a family is living collectively. It's just a very restricted form of it.'⁹ One function of family living for capitalism, he argues, is to contain our innate desire for collectivity within a unit that is often chauvinistic, competitive and exclusionary.

Most depictions of the nuclear household portray a nestled harmony. But for many, the experience of 'home' – and of 'stay at home' – is one of stress and unsafety. The nuclear household is the primary site of violence and oppression against women and children. It is where queer and trans people, whose existence threatens the heteronormative order, experience torture, rejection and ejection. According to the charity Stonewall, more than a quarter of trans people have suffered domestic violence and a quarter have experienced homelessness.¹⁰

Within this kind of home, women in heterosexual relationships, or single mothers with children, are typically burdened with most of the unpaid labour of social reproduction: the caring, cooking and cleaning that keeps people alive and well enough to work another day. 'STAY HOME. SAVE LIVES', announced a government advert depicting three women cleaning and looking after children, and one man relaxing on the sofa.¹¹ Housework, writes Sylvia Federici in 'Wages against Housework', is 'the most pervasive manipulation, the most subtle and mystified violence that capitalism has ever perpetrated against any section of the working class'.¹²

In the nuclear household, 'women's work' has been naturalised and invisiblised, writes Federici:

In the same way as god created Eve to give pleasure to Adam, so did capital create the housewife to service the male worker physically, emotionally and sexually – to raise his children, mend his socks, patch up his ego when it is crushed by the work and the social relations (which are relations of loneliness) that capital has reserved for him. It is precisely this peculiar combination of physical, emotional and sexual services that are involved in the role women must perform for capital that creates the specific character of that servant which is the housewife, that makes her work so burdensome and at the same time invisible. It is not an accident that most men start thinking of getting married as soon as they get their first job.[13]

No wonder then, that whilst older men today are likely to desire cohabitation with a woman – with the companionship, care and health benefits this will statistically entail – studies show that older women are more likely than men to choose to live alone.[*]

Rich women, of course, have always had less to worry about when it comes to the burden of domestic labour, having the option to hire 'help'. In what Sophie Lewis calls 'an extractive hierarchy of outsourced wife-work',[14] wealthy families routinely employ poorer women – often immigrant and racialised – to do housework and childcare. Only rich, mostly white, women win by outsourcing drudgery.

Liberal feminists, however, might celebrate this option, as they did in a Covid-era Twitter debate over the 'right to a cleaner'. After the journalist Owen Jones tweeted encouraging middle-class people to pay their cleaners to stay at home during the pandemic, *Spectator* columnist Sarah

---

[*] For example, in the United States, the 'Older Americans 2016' report by the Federal Interagency Forum on Aging-Related Statistics showed that unmarried women do much better emotionally and physically than unmarried men of a similar age, and that among people over 75, women were twice as likely as men to live alone.

Ditum responded saying that cleaning over lockdown was 'KILLING' her. Ditum and other self-proclaimed feminists rallied to argue that cleaners gained self-esteem from their work, and that such work gave working-class women's lives a sense of purpose. In reality of course, at best, working allows working-class women to survive. At worst, it makes them sick – for instance, because of unsafe workplaces at the height of a pandemic – or kills them. This social order is enduring: in Paris in 1918, a quarter of the women who died during the Spanish Flu pandemic were servants. At times of acute crisis, it becomes abundantly clear that social reproduction is the work that keeps life going when everything is falling apart: who does it, and under what conditions, are essential questions.

The hostile home we are sold

Even at its best, the nuclear or private household is rarely the cosy haven it is touted as. The cultural messaging that glorifies home as a place of relaxation, tenderness and unity might evoke a certain longing – perhaps because, for most of us, it is a fiction.

The state's preferred model of homelife is not privileged for its likelihood to foster love and happiness, but for its utility to capital. 'The normative (monoracial, heterosexual, nuclear) household, though increasingly rare, is the foundation of statist futurity', write the Out of the Woods (OOTW) collective. 'It is perhaps the key institution in (re)producing citizens loyal to property, nation, and race.'[15] This understanding of home, they write, is driven by what Angela Mitropoulos identifies as 'oikonomics': 'the nexus of race, gender, class, sexuality and nation constituted through the premise of the properly productive household'.[16] Organising society into atomised units like this props up the reproduction of workers for capitalism, shores up property relations through marriage and inheritance, and restricts opportunities for solidarity against the state. Private households maximise consumption whilst minimising communality – for example, from the mid-twentieth century, the rise of domestic appliances marketed at women saw a shift away from shared services such as laundrettes.

Many groups are excluded from this limited and limiting vision of home. People without a home or living in a version of home other than the capitalist ideal are maligned and disciplined or deprived of housing altogether as a punishment for alterity. Drug users are routinely excluded from shelters; queer and trans people struggle to find safe refuge; undocumented migrants face criminalisation if they seek shelter, such as when the homeless charity St Mungo's colluded with the Home Office to identify migrants for deportation, as revealed by *The Guardian* in 2018.[17] Meanwhile, rough sleepers face stigma and cruelty for attempting to survive on the streets – especially those who drink alcohol, despite the fact the housed population might think nothing of their own bottle-of-wine-a-night habit, in 'the privacy of their own home'.

Those who live in households at odds with the state – such as in Gypsy, Roma and Traveller (GRT) communities – are subjected to state violence and racism. Nomadism has been made increasingly difficult due to diminishing legal stopping places, and barriers to employment, healthcare and education whilst moving around. However, whilst there are almost no legal stopping places, in order to be considered part of an 'ethnic group' under the law, with the supposed protection this entails, GRTs *must* remain nomadic.

In a 2015 interview, campaigner Shay Clipson told me that the government's treatment of GRT communities was 'ethnic cleansing, no guns or bloodshed, but it's the iron fist in the velvet glove, making it impossible for people to exist and practise their cultural way of life'.[18] There is a lot of evidence, she says, that GRTs forced into bricks and mortar houses suffer psychological harms. And things have only gotten worse since then. In 2021, Labour MP Charlotte Nichols canvassed using leaflets announcing a racist pledge to 'deal with traveller incursions'.* The Police, Crime, Sentencing and Courts (PCSC) Act is intensifying attacks, targeting GRTs even further. Despite a severe lack of provision by local authorities for legal sites, the Act criminalises 'unauthorised encampments', handing the police additional powers of enforcement. Such 'enforcement' against GRT homes can involve a £2,500 fine, prison time, or the 'confiscation' of home and belongings.

The dominant ideology of home has its foundations in white nationalism. As bell hooks asserts: 'An effective means of white subjugation of black people globally has been the perpetual construction of economic and social structures that deprive many folks of the means to make homeplace.'[19] In the eyes of the state, 'home' is not something everybody deserves, but a privilege that may be denied or stripped away. Who is allowed to make their home in the UK, and who is subjected to state violence if they attempt to? In 2012, the then Home Secretary Theresa May's 'hostile environment' policy sought to make the nation so inhospitable and immiserating to migrants that they would 'go home'. In 2013, a Home Office advertising campaign saw vans emblazoned with 'GO HOME OR FACE ARREST' driven around London boroughs with high migrant populations, while passport checks were introduced in hospitals and schools. Even those who had already 'legally' made their home in the UK, including people of the Windrush Generation, were denied rights in healthcare and employment, and faced detention and deportation. The racist climate of suspicion and hate fostered by such policies has led

---

* After criticism, Nichols apologised and withdrew the leaflet from circulation.

to countless deaths, as medical attention, housing and work have become more difficult to access safely, or at all.

Hostile environment policies rage on today, having recently been consolidated in the Nationality and Borders Act. The new law is designed to prevent people seeking life-saving refuge from exercising their right to asylum in the UK. In violation of international law, the Nationality and Borders Act states that people who enter the UK without permission will be criminalised – facing imprisonment and a suspension of their full right to asylum. Those helping others to reach the UK safely – even not 'for gain' – can now face criminal prosecution. Meanwhile, until the proposed policy was withdrawn in April 2022 thanks to legal challenges, the government planned to give the UK Border Force immunity from conviction if 'pushback' operations led to refugees drowning. And for asylum seekers who do make it to the UK – as of this year, the government is threatening to 'remove' them to Rwanda. The burgeoning terror of the climate crisis will intensify fascist border regimes – denying yet more people the refuge of home and the opportunity to live.

The 'race-family-nation nexus centered on the household', argue the OOTW collective, is invoked by states seeking to 'ramp up border panic and demand more border violence', showing how 'supposedly unrelated struggles around social reproduction are in fact critical in contesting the reproduction of unconscious racial investments'.[21]

The unhomeliness of home

Contrary to the popular imaginary – in pandemic advertising, in festive imagery, in romantic films – home as we know it is not a source of indiscriminate unity. The nuclear household can foment isolation, crushing the potential of expansive intimacies and solidarities. And, in the fractures of home, capital percolates, flogging objects designed to pacify us.

The uncomradely insularity of modern homes increasingly takes the form of interpersonal surveillance, or 'smart security'. For example, the 'Amazon Ring' doorbell records a home's immediate surroundings, building a private surveillance network accessible to connected smartphones – as well as the police. Ring users can send recordings to other users, sharing information about 'suspicious' people and activity. In 2020, an Amazon software engineer wrote to management saying the technology is 'simply not compatible with a free society'.[22]

Even though household burglaries have become far rarer over the past 20 years,[23] the rise of private surveillance technology like this stokes feelings of mistrust among neighbours, leading more and more people to turn to such products to feel 'safe'. Despite hacking incidents and a recent court ruling that the Ring contributed to harassment and was in breach of data protection laws, sales continue to rise.[24] Now, Amazon patents show that it is developing doorbells that not only capture audio and video but also detect 'suspicious' people's identities based on their gait, skin texture, voice and even odour.[25] In a white supremacist society, biometric assessments such as this codify racism. Home surveillance systems like the Ring are attracting burgeoning criticism from civil liberties groups, as they automate racist policing, turning neighbourhoods into cop terrain and those who live close to us into potential informants.

In a society where many would-be homes are vacant and many inhabited houses are hollow, we seek solace in empty places. Clothing brands imitate belonging; 'hygge' interiors simulate comfort; workplaces adopt a home-like façade of sofas and fruit bowls. Mobile phones can numb us to our dislocation whilst we are in their grip; our scrolling might feel homeward bound. According to a University College London study of their use across the world, phones have become our 'transportal home'. When people 'retreat' into their mobiles, the researchers write, they have 'in effect, gone home' – to familiar activities, images and communities.[26] Indeed, virtual domesticities might feel all the more alluring on our unstable planetary home – and yet the very manufacturing of our phone-homes contributes to the ecological crisis, just as their use can tranquilise us to its urgency.

As the market offers us ever more remedies for rootlessness, we might ask what these short-term fixes could do to the possibility of finding spiritual grounding, in the communal, with those living around us.

To be at home in resistance

We are living in a time of 'domestic realism', claims feminist scholar Helen Hester, defined as 'the phenomenon by which the isolated and individualized small dwelling (and the concomitant privatization of household labor) becomes so accepted and commonplace that it is nearly impossible to imagine life being organized in any other way'.[27] This 'realism', she argues, is all the more remarkable considering that many people's lived experience of this kind of home is marked by an unreasonable amount of suffering.

Those bearing the brunt of the dominant logic of home, however – those forced to suffer most within it, or who are expelled from it – have always organised against it, and built alternative homes, in search of security, care and belonging. Our task now, argues Lewis, is 'to restore the private (repro-normative or patriarchal) nuclear household to its proper place as the principal object of feminist and queer radical critique'.[28] This struggle, she suggests, could be named 'Real homes against the home'.[29]

The Wages for Housework campaign called for the recognition of domestic labour as work under capitalism, refuting the idea that the nuclear household exists because of women's 'love' alone:

> To say that we want wages for housework is to expose the fact that housework is already money for capital, that capital has made and makes money out of our cooking, smiling, fucking. At the same time, it shows that we have cooked, smiled, fucked throughout the years not because it was easier for us than for anybody else, but because we did not have any other choice.[30]

The campaign was a political standpoint, built on class solidarity; it demanded that 'women's work' be recognised as such, as part of a wider struggle to revolutionise personal, social and economic relations. 'We are seen as nagging bitches, not workers in struggle', wrote Federici.[31] In this way, she argued, the fury of the 'privatised kitchen-bedroom quarrel that all society agrees to ridicule' must be galvanised into *workplace* demands; the 'housewife' would be an agitator for radical change.[32]

Today, women and others most oppressed and exploited in private households follow in the footsteps of the Wages for Housework campaign – for example, the women's strike movement calls for the refusal of all work traditionally done by women and challenges patriarchal trade union organising, which usually overlooks feminised labour.

Showing solidarity with migrants is another avenue for disrupting the 'oikonomic' home, whose essence is calcified in the *Home* Office. In May 2021, on the first day of Eid, Glaswegians united against Immigration Enforcement to block a raid that sought to remove people from their homes and deport them in the midst of the pandemic. Two hundred protesters resisted the Home Office van – chanting 'these are our neighbours, let them go' – which resulted in two men being released back into their community. Migrant solidarity has a powerful history in Glasgow. Since the arrival of asylum seekers towards the end of the 1990s, the Unity Centre – situated near the Scottish Home Office – has been fighting alongside them. The Centre not only resists deportations and offers support with paperwork, it also provides – as one activist speaking to *The Guardian* put it – 'emotional solidarity', hoping to support migrants to *feel* at home. Glasgow city council has also paired asylum seekers with neighbours, so they receive a warm welcome. And when the Home Office has attempted to 'remove' their new friends in dawn raids, Glaswegians have refused to allow it.[33]

Homes configured around queerness, too, could pose a threat to domination and violence. As Lauren Berlant writes, 'queer spaces' have been fundamental to building a less homophobic world, because 'otherwise, non-normative sexualities have, during the twentieth century, mainly represented negative forms of social value, establishing a boundary through taboo and terror that has helped to prop up heterosexual culture'.[34]

A queer home might be stable or transitory. It might mean communal domesticity, or simply a place that evokes affinity. A good party – where people feel free and nurtured – can feel like home-as-joyful-defiance. Queer nightlife during the AIDS pandemic not only offered pleasurable escape, but formed part of a community care strategy; Notting Hill Carnival was borne of Black resistance to racist violence during the 1950s. The New York ballroom scene – with its opulent events where people 'walk' in competitions, and its chosen family 'houses' – provides, as Judith Butler once suggested in an interview, 'a great subversive rearticulation of houseness', in that 'A "house" is the people you "walk" with.'[35]

Going against the mainstream, it can be hard for counter-current homes to endure – especially when they defy the logic of private property. From the late 1960s to the 1980s, 'home' and political organising became entwined in new and generative ways, with the rise of squatting alongside gay and women's liberation movements. In squatting uninhabited buildings, people take their 'human right' to housing* into their own hands, rather than facing the streets, local authority waiting lists or bankrupting rents. Squats are not only central to political organising against the conditions that lead to poverty and homelessness in the first place, they are also places where people shut out from or harmed by traditional 'home life' – whether for lack of resources or because of their identity – can explore other ways of living. Such homes might encompass 'homeplace', as described by hooks: places 'where we can recover ourselves' and create 'a community of resistance'.[36]

Communal living during the 1960s, '70s and '80s – in squats or otherwise – partly reflected a certain contemporaneous utopian spirit. It was also down to more affordable property: in her memoir, revolutionary feminist Sheila Rowbotham recounts buying a communal house in Dalston, Hackney in the 1960s, whilst in her twenties – something people of comparable relative earnings could only dream of today.[37]

Some communal homes grew out of specific political movements. Over the course of the 1970s, Gay Liberation Front (GLF) communes across London pushed back against the binaries of cisheteronormativity and the nuclear household, becoming hubs for the exploration of gender and sexuality. In 1974, the GLF squatted 78 Railton Road in Brixton, opening the UK's first gay community centre, surrounded by other squats, which held parties, knitting circles, exercise

---

* The right to adequate housing is included in the 1948 Universal Declaration of Human Rights.

classes and film screenings, and ran a gay helpline. Railton Road housed outcasts and revolutionaries of many sorts; it was a hub for activism, solidarity and mutual aid, and a riotous experiment in and against an authoritarian state. At different points, the street was home to women's centres, squatters' support groups, the National Gay News Defence Committee, the Anarchist News Service, a claimants' union, a radical gay counselling group and the Race Today Collective, which published a journal on Black politics.

Meanwhile, East London became a nucleus for women-only and lesbian communes, where women organised politically, made art together and collectivised their lives, including the care of children. In 1973, a group of gender-nonconforming feminist queers in Bethnal Green set up the 'Bethnal Rogue' acid drag commune, which was both a living space and a queer bookshop. The nearby London Fields area is estimated to have been home to over 50 feminist households.

Following in the footsteps of the 1970s squats – especially the first women's refuge, which squatted Palm Court Hotel in Richmond in 1975 – in 2016, the feminist group Sisters Uncut, which protests for well-funded domestic violence services, reclaimed an empty council flat in Hackney and turned it into a community centre.

The history of squatting and communal living in Britain is also the history of anti-racist survival and resistance. Occupying empty buildings can be a way to build homes in defiance of the racist state and to facilitate organising against it. In 1972, Liz Obi and Olive Morris, squatters' rights activists and members of the Brixton Black Panthers, occupied 121 Railton Road, founding a squat – with a disco in the cellar – that was used by Black radicals, anarchists and feminists for decades to come. In the 1970s too, Bangladeshi squatters made their homes in empty properties in East London, leading to the creation of the Bengali Housing Action Group.

Squats and communes like those that grew up in the 1970s present a different vision of what it might mean to 'be at home'. Collective living – especially in spaces seized by occupation – sees the meaning of 'home' transformed. A radical home is not a secluded private property for a select few bound by blood. Rather than being a bunker, it is a network of care; not lifelessly compliant, but the embodiment of demands. As Paul Jackson suggests, this kind of home is not even necessarily a physical space, 'but a process to make more and more kinship'.[38] For the incarcerated, 'home' may be a struggle and a longing for places they are unable to be, things they are unable to do and people they are unable to touch.

A radical home may be an example of what English professor Susan Fraiman calls 'extreme domesticity'. In this understanding, the domestic is not the domain of the patriarchal private household, but something that those most marginalised by it create. The 'extreme' domestic has multiple meanings:

> extreme as a reference to dire circumstances due to such things as economic insecurity, physical vulnerability, and/or stigmatized identity; extreme in the sense of balancing on a knife-edge, as in X-treme sports; extreme in the sense of being seen as immoderate or outlandish; extreme in the sense of gender/sexuality that is shunned as X-rated, offensive to 'family values' and off-limits to children; and extreme in the sense of occupying an eccentric position vis-á-vis the center, being on the outskirts of belonging, including the exilic state of being without national, marital, or other social standing.[39]

In increasingly harsh circumstances – including the housing crisis, and the sharpening criminalisation of rough sleeping and political activism – extreme domesticity persists today. Everywhere, people are homemaking out of the rubble.

The Outside Project is a London LGBTIQ+ community shelter, centre and domestic abuse refuge, opened in 2017 and run by grassroots activists, including those with experience of homelessness. It is a place for 'those within the LGBTIQ+ community who feel endangered, who are homeless, "hidden" homeless and feel that they are on the outside of services due to historical and present prejudice in society and in their homes'.[40] The shelter offers people their own rooms, with access to support workers and activities including photography, meditation and walking groups. In 2020, The Outside Project started the Emergency Hotel and Outreach service, which provided rooms for homeless LGBTIQ+ people during the pandemic, and the STAR Refuge, for LGBTIQ+ people fleeing domestic abuse.

In as much as the pandemic has shone a spotlight on the inadequacies and harms of the housing system and households as we know them, it has also catalysed revindications of home. The often tragic inadequacy of individualising households has become undeniable even to proponents of the nuclear family. As the virus spread, mutual aid groups, street kitchens and local food co-ops sprung up across the UK (and the world), building networks of social reproduction to reduce people's suffering in (and without) isolated homes. Amid the crisis, collaboration and reciprocity – rooted in anarchist organising principles – suddenly made more sense than top-down 'charity'.

As millions lost their jobs and wages during pandemic lockdowns, an unprecedented number of people were unable to hand over money to landlords to keep a roof over their heads. On the day the government lifted the eviction ban in May 2021, around 5 per cent of renters were at risk of eviction, with many more fearing homelessness in the months to come. Eviction resistance surged. In June 2021, our neighbour mobilised her local community when she and her three children faced homelessness or forced relocation by the council to accommodation 170 miles away. Around 80 of us – including from renters' unions and our local food co-op, which started during the pandemic – gathered to stop the repossession. The action bought the family some time, and the organising group that built around it continued to fight alongside her in her struggle to remain in her lifelong home locality.

The pandemic, too, saw a resurgence of the rent strike movement, in which students led the way. In 2020, in the largest win in UK student rent strike history, strikers at the University of Manchester won a 30 per cent rent reduction, worth £12 million. Even after this win, the strikers held strong for their other demands, including improved facilities, services and mental health support, changes to campus security and policing, and tuition fee refunds. The nationwide wave of rent strikes has also led some students to think seriously about building homes that don't rely upon paying rent; student housing co-ops are seeing a revival.

In recent years, there have also been a number of militant occupations, including as part of the Kill The Bill movement, resisting the PCSC Bill, and the fortifying struggle for police abolition. In March 2021, activists squatted the former Clapham Common police station in opposition to the PCSC Bill, in the wake of the murder of Sarah Everard by police officer Wayne Couzens. In a statement posted on Instagram, the group, citing the 1.5 million empty properties in the UK, wrote: 'We occupied this former cop shop because police represent the epitome of violent white supremacist, patriarchal capitalism that protects property over people … We firmly believe in reclaiming and repurposing empty spaces as social centres, homes and for the practice of mutual aid within the community.'[41] Whilst fighting off police harassment and eviction threats, the group held socially distanced outdoor workshops, including a self-defence class for women and non-binary people, and political education sessions.

In the winter of 2021, a group of houseless people squatted the former St Mungo's Hostel on Gray's Inn Road, London, to form the Autonomous Winter Shelter. In a statement, the squatters said:

> People shouldn't be forced to freeze to death on the streets of a country that has chosen to forget them. Rising rent costs and continuous lack of compassion from the services set up to help has enabled a widespread blind eye for those in situations like these – it's time we worked from the ground up. None of us should be one missed paycheck away from homelessness – and none of us should be sleeping rough in the middle of winter. We must show solidarity with our own communities ... We are sick of sombre spaces and half-assed hostels. Instead, we are taking direct action – organising to assist each other in times of crisis.[42]

All these examples of 'home' counterpose the dominant ideology of the household by, at once, resisting its oppressions and offering up new homely possibilities, refusing the walls of private property and the state. In this way, as the OOTW collective write, 'kinship is figured not through biological proximity nor geographical adjacency, rather it is expressed through a shared relation to the world such that whoever exists within it lives in an affective, affectable closeness, holding and supporting one another'.[43] This kind of kinship-in-action, they argue, 'disrupts the oikonomic operations', encompassing 'all refusals of the reproductive-futurist nexus of race-family-nation'.[44] For many – especially working-class, migrant and queer people – 'home' is demanding: both in the sense that it is difficult, and in that it can entail radical demands. Doing social reproduction beyond the nuclear or private household builds networks of care that, in their very existence, unsettle the foundations of the hegemonic household.

There's no place like home

Everyone deserves housing, and home is something we make together. The potential of home, however, is to a large extent determined by our social realities and the resources we have access to. Having good and reliable shelter necessitates a certain level of financial security; being able to escape and find refuge from a miserable or unsafe household requires a safety net. Utopian ideas alone will not fix the unhappy state of 'home' – in its material impossibility for many, in its gendered oppression and violence, in its abuse of queer people, in its privation of community. But the political demands expressed through experiments in living – like homes for all, communalised resources, queer liberation, no borders – can lay powerful foundations for a future of abundant homeliness, especially when such explorations foster powerful intimacy alongside conspiration. Our biggest challenge in 'doing home differently' might be, as Fisher suggests, 'making it stick over time',[45] practising the commitment and persistence that families often do so doggedly. Whilst radical homes might welcome flexibility, people need some consistency to feel secure enough.

Imagination is essential. How will we inspire ourselves towards homemaking, towards a future in which we are all at home? In the 1970s queer utopian text *The Faggots & Their Friends Between Revolutions*, Larry Mitchell paints a glorious picture of the home of 'the tribe of Angel Flesh':

The house of Angel Flesh is old, elaborate and slightly tilted. Vines completely cover the crumbling porches. Inside is misty, hung with soft fabrics, and smells of jasmine and the sacred substances. Lilac was, when he entered for the first time, immediately calm. Each room in the house is devoted to a different living form. One is filled with velvets and feathers and make-up and sparkles and costumes and silks. It is where the faggots go when they want to transform themselves. Another room is for plants to live in; another is for quiet music; another is for silent eating; and another is for methodically drinking teas of healing herbs. All who live there move softly about the house, living all through it. At night they sleep all together in the central room of the house. The fire glows over the large pillows that cover the floor with the tribe covering the pillows. … They learned to heal each other by saying magic words over and over again and they learned to bring loving vibrations to the body to make it strong again. All this they share with all those around them who want to know. Each night in the big central room of the house, when sleep comes, they hold each other until they hardly know where one of them stops and another one begins. [46]

Radical homes take living together consensually, in freedom and pleasure, seriously. In *The Dialectic of Sex*, Shulamith Firestone envisioned households that grow up around 'ten or so consenting adults', agreeing to a licence, renewed perhaps every seven to ten years, or however long it was decided the children in the household needed 'a stable structure in which to grow up'.[47] In this kind of household, she proposed, children would not belong to their parents, but would be free to move to another household if they were unhappy in the one into which they 'had been born so arbitrarily'.[48] More recently, Lewis has called for the family abolitionist 'gestational commune', in which children are de-commodified and collaboratively produced, care is collectivised and comradeship supersedes competition.[49]

CHAPTER FIVE

The great equaliser

We will be known as a culture that feared death
and adored power, that tried to vanquish insecurity
for the few and cared little for the penury of the
many…

Mary Oliver

riots are a work of vast and incomprehensible mourning
Sean Bonney

The 2021 global climate change summit, COP26 in Glasgow, Scotland, was a meeting about death from which those facing the most mortal threat were systemically excluded. The conference happened against the backdrop of the Covid-19 pandemic, which meant that the barriers to attendance for people on the frontline of ecological crisis in the Global South, already facing the racist border regime, were exceptionally high. According to the COP26 Coalition, a UK-based civil society network mobilising around climate justice, a large proportion of those who had intended to come to Glasgow from the Global South were unable to, in part due to the inaccessibility of vaccines. Both the climate and the Covid-19 crises – and their collision at COP26 – demonstrate the deadly impact of racial capitalism, in which the profit motive supersedes the value ascribed to certain lives.

Capitalism is inhuman in that – beyond there being enough people able to keep profit flowing upwards – it does not matter to the system whether we, individually, live or die. But within this system, some lives are worth more than others; capitalist expansion depends upon rendering some lives disposable. Capitalism is, as the philosopher and political theorist Achille Mbembe describes, 'necropolitical' – it entails the 'subjugation of life to the power of death', building what he calls 'death-worlds': 'forms of social existence in which vast populations are subjected to conditions of life conferring upon them the status of *living dead*'.[1]

As rich nations prioritising corporate interests blocked access to life-saving Covid-19 vaccines in the Global South, in turn preventing people from communities on the front-line of the ecological crisis from attending COP26, they also obstructed a climate agreement that could have saved lives the world over – especially those most at risk from climate change. Of the COP26 agreement, Indigenous climate activist Thomas Joseph said: 'The leaders pushing for market-based solutions and the commodification of our Mother Earth are signing a death sentence.'[2]

Capitalism is killing us

For some people, capitalism might feel like a wily murderer, gradually sapping the life out of bodies and souls through unrelenting stress. For others, its murderousness is more immediate and brutal. The uneven death toll under capitalism plays out at all scales – including within, at and across the deadly borders of the UK. Working-class and racialised people in the UK face disproportionate threats from the climate crisis, for example. Structural inequalities mean they are more likely to breathe air with unlawful levels of pollution and are more likely to face homelessness because of extreme weather events, due to low-quality housing.

The years of the pandemic have underscored the ways in which systemic oppression and state violence narrate mortality. Covid-19 deaths are raced and classed and have exposed society's grave ableism. People in prisons and detention centres have been left to die, or to live in deathlike conditions – with prisoners, for example, being locked in their cells for all but 60 minutes each day. Low-wage frontline workers, Black and brown people and disabled people have all lost their lives disproportionately during the pandemic. Some workers have been forced to labour throughout, in unsafe conditions, scarce personal protective equipment and inadequate sick pay intensifying the threat of infection. And when it came to treating those with Covid-19, it soon became evident that disabled people's lives would not be treated with the same sanctity. Some Covid-19 patients with learning disabilities, for instance, were given 'do not resuscitate' notices.

As the pandemic was taking hold, in May 2020, George Floyd was murdered by white police officer Derek Chauvin in the United States. The Black Lives Matter movement took to the streets all over the world, demanding that the white supremacist institution of policing be demolished, and that Black lives be protected. In England and Wales, since 1990, there have been almost 2,000 deaths in police custody or otherwise following contact with the police.[3] According to the charity Inquest – which campaigns and advocates on state-related deaths – the proportion of 'Black, Asian and Minoritised Ethnicities (BAME)' deaths in custody where restraint or force was a factor is more than double that of other deaths in custody.

Police violence, this time against women, also made the headlines and sparked protest in March 2021 in the UK, following the abduction, rape and murder of Sarah Everard by Wayne Couzens, a white Metropolitan police officer who had formerly worked as a parliamentary guard, and who used Covid laws to abduct Everard. After her disappearance, police characteristically responsiblised women for patriarchal violence, advising them to stay indoors at night. The previous year in June, two white Metropolitan police officers, Deniz Jaffer and Jamie Lewis, took selfies of themselves with the corpses of Nicole Smallman and Bibaa Henry, two Black women who had been murdered in a London park, before sharing them in a police officer WhatsApp group, calling the victims 'dead birds'.

Death is certain for us all – but who dies when and how, in what conditions, with what care, is a question of politics.

The 'great equaliser'?

The deathly violence of global capitalism and the state plays out in gradual as well as sudden ways. Most people die of 'natural causes' – which is to say a coroner has ruled out an 'external cause'. This verdict is, in many ways, misleading. With the conditions of our lives being so tied up with the structures and mechanisms of capitalism, can our deaths ever be 'natural' and free of 'external causes'? As both the pandemic and the climate crisis demonstrate, 'natural' deaths can be directly linked to the global economy. And whilst people are living longer overall, sickness, healthcare, ageing, end-of-life care and death look very different depending on who you are and where you are. Life expectancy in the London borough of Westminster is ten years higher than in Glasgow.[4] Tory-linked private healthcare companies selling costly medical check-ups – such as Randox* – advertise using slogans like 'EXTEND YOUR LIFE'.[5]

Government policy determines life chances. As Philip Alston, the UN rapporteur on extreme poverty and human

---

* The Tory government awarded Randox almost £800m worth of Covid-19 testing contracts.

rights, wrote in his report on the impact of austerity in the UK in 2019:

> Although the United Kingdom is the world's fifth largest economy, one fifth of its population (14 million people) live in poverty, and 1.5 million of them experienced destitution in 2017 ... Close to 40 per cent of children are predicted to be living in poverty by 2021. Food banks have proliferated; homelessness and rough sleeping have increased greatly; tens of thousands of poor families must live in accommodation far from their schools, jobs and community networks; life expectancy is falling for certain groups; and the legal aid system has been decimated.[6]

Austerity, he wrote, adopted 'a harsh and uncaring ethos' and an ideological approach to policy that has 'tragic social consequences'.[7]

Many people who are unwell or disabled go without proper care. Indeed, it is difficult, even, to convince the government that you are not 'fit to work', in order to access any state support at all. Those whose health means they are unable or unwilling to work are subject to a 'scroungers' and 'shirkers' narrative – rhetoric propelled by successive governments to invoke disdain for those without paid employment among those with jobs. Meanwhile, inaccessible and meagre benefits and low or nonexistent sick pay force people to work when it poses health risks.

Toxic work culture, like many aspects of our lives under capitalism, ruins our health as it ruins our world – in turn making us sicker, whilst we are obliged to be well enough to labour on. The ways we mine the planet, manufacture commodities and are herded into certain lifestyles make us, along with the planet, unwell. As Audre Lorde wrote of her cancer diagnosis in the 1980s:

I'm not being paranoid when I say my cancer is as political as if some CIA agent brushed past me in the A train
on March 15, 1965, and air-injected me with a long-fused
cancer virus ... What possible choices do most of us have in
the air we breathe and the water we must drink?[8]

More recently, the poet Anne Boyer wrote of her cancer: 'It is
as if I am both sick with and treated by the twentieth century,
its weapons and pesticides, its epic generalizations and its
expensive festivals of death. Then, sick beyond sick from that
century, I am made sick, again, from information – a sickness
that is our century's own.'[9] The cancer treatments she was
receiving, notes Boyer, have ecological implications; the price
of her own individual getting better, she is aware, is making
other living beings sick. Such is life under capitalism.

What about plain old dying from being old? Surely some
things are sacred? Certainly, people are getting on. There are
now – for the first time ever – more people over the age of
65 in the world than under five.[10] In 2019, one-fifth of the
UK population was 65 or over. By 2043, people over 65 are
expected to make up a quarter of the population overall.[11]

People living longer lives, however, does not necessarily
mean more years of health and enjoyment. To match increasing life expectancies, the state increases retirement age rather
than investing in provision for longer retirements. In today's
economic climate, increasing numbers of people likely won't
be able to afford to retire at all, or to afford care when they
need it.

Dementia and Alzheimer's disease are the leading causes of
death in the UK, and the most financially devastating. The
so-called 'dementia tax' means that people unwell in this way
– who are more likely to require social care rather than free
hospital care, and for longer – are burdened with care bills
that the Alzheimer's Society estimates would take the average

person 125 years to save for.[12] Social care is in crisis due to underfunding, privatisation and financialisation. In the context of the United States, but just as relevant to the UK, the historian Gabriel Winant writes that, given the escalating care crisis as well as those in housing and welfare, we will be facing a future of 'homeless shelters packed with octogenarians' unless we act now.[13]

Millions of people have unmet care needs that make daily life a struggle, whilst for care workers, poor conditions, precarious contracts and poverty wages prevail. Professional carers – of which there are around 1.5 million, many of whom have personal care responsibilities, too – are critically overworked and underpaid. According to 2021 analysis by the Trade Union Congress, 70 per cent of carers – mostly women, many of whom are migrants – earn less than £10 per hour.[14] Unpaid carers meanwhile – usually friends and family caring for people in their homes – are possibly eligible for a 'carer's allowance' of just £69.70 per week, *if they care for someone for at least 35 hours a week*. Around 1.3 million people claim this unliveable allowance.

In this landscape, the Covid-19 pandemic has underscored the fallacy of dying of 'natural causes'. Not only did systemic vulnerabilities and crumbling state infrastructure lead to scores of avoidable deaths, but the origin of the pathogen itself is likely linked to the ecological crisis born out of the economic system.

What's wrong with dying?

Though every day we all get older, and death is as inexorable as breathing, we mostly look away from our own mortality. Perhaps, as Susan Sontag posited, 'One can't look steadily at death any more than one can stare at the sun.'[15] But whilst fearing death may seem to be a universal life experience, our orientation towards ageing and end-of-life is historically and culturally specific, rendered along lines of class, race, gender and religion. How a society approaches death might reflect the dominant ideologies with which it approaches life.

As death studies historian Kami Fletcher writes, European settler colonialism – 'via slavery, war, and genocide – marginalized, trivialized, and outright negated deathways* and death practices, of nations, cultures and persons deemed "other"'.[16] What are held up as common-sense beliefs and practices around death in the UK today are linked to the histories and ongoing realities of colonialism – including white supremacy and the violent imposition of Christianity and capitalist cultures.

The way we understand death influences how we relate to older people. In general, intergenerational mixing is not facilitated or encouraged. For most of our lives, unless we have proximate relationships with our immediate relatives, older age is 'somewhere else'. A 2020 study by the Centre for Ageing Better found that the UK – in popular stereotypes and in the media, for example – demonstrates an 'ingrained culture' of 'pity and dislike' towards older people. The research found that ageism impacts some groups more than others, with people from Black and minority ethnic groups and women facing a 'double jeopardy' of ageist discrimination.[17]

Older people experience disproportionate levels of isolation and loneliness. Around 40 per cent of people over 75 in the UK live alone, and older people with high care needs are more likely to receive care from a paid stranger in their private home or in a care home than to be cared for by loved ones sharing the responsibility.

---

* Fletcher defines 'deathways' as 'ways of dying which can also include burial practices, funerals, mourning, corpse care'.

According to charity Age UK, one in 12 older adults report being lonely often, a number projected to increase.[18] In a society that locates caring responsibility primarily within nuclear families, this is unsurprising. Whilst society is set up so that older people may depend upon family care, if they indeed have a family to speak of, society is also organised and paced so that this kind of care – which in a different world people might long to do out of love – can be a devastating or impossible obligation. This immense pressure upon immediate biological family often leads to the breakdown of relationships, for example those of siblings. The care deficit so many people experience is not a unilateral cruelty, but a nightmare facing everyone. The idea that we ourselves may go uncared for at the end of our lives is a terrifying reckoning. As Sophie Lewis notes, 'lonely, fearful, disenfranchised deaths, in turn, breed trauma among the living'.[19]

Via denial, dominant culture fetishises youth. Whilst children and young people are denied agency, the fantasy of early adulthood is 'living your best life' – being flawless, sprightly, hot, uninhibited! Even though the material conditions of young adults' lives are likely to be worse than those of their parents – they are less likely to have secure housing and work, for example – and even though they have been born into mounting global and societal crises, young adults are supposed to prosper. Whilst the young might find many good reasons to fear for their future lives, the very fact of their relative distance from old age is supposed to be an enviable, peak experience.

The cultural fascination with youth is expressed through a fixation on the body's largest organ, skin – which might give clues to ourselves and those perceiving us as to our proximity to death. It has been claimed that people are more likely to stop smoking for fear of its aesthetic (ageing) impacts, rather than the ways it damages internal organs making us likely to actually die sooner. The rise of 'skincare regimes', instructional make-up videos and injectable fillers attests to the importance ascribed to a baby-faced sheen. *Looking* young and healthy, even when we are not, is rewarded. As Boyer writes of meeting a friend whilst she has cancer: 'On that day, I do everything to look healthy so that my friend will praise the skillfulness of my camouflage, its materials purchased at Wigs.com, CVS, and Sephora.'[20] She refers to 'look good feel better' workshops, supported by the – often 'pinkwashing'* – cosmetics industry, which teach cancer patients to cover up 'areas of concern'.[21]

As subjects in modern capitalism, we are urged to 'take care of ourselves' – to self-preserve – by beauty brands and our bosses, rather than just by those who would actually suffer if we became seriously unwell or died. We are urged to put work into, as Erich Fromm put it, 'camouflaging death'.[22]

We are led to believe – more so as women – that to be young, healthy and beautiful is to be loveable and desirable. The fact that – according to ableist, racist, transphobic, fat-phobic and conventional beauty standards – many of us will never be all three, then, may be profoundly distressing. It has become a popular feminist insistence that we only or primarily tend to our appearance 'for ourselves'. But if we were guaranteed of a lifetime of cherishing love no matter how we looked, would we really spend so much time and money 'optimising our assets'?

The biotech industry is seeking a 'cure' for ageing itself. The US military are conducting trials of an anti-ageing pill

---

* 'Pinkwashing' in this sense was coined in 2002 by the US campaign group Breast Cancer Action, to refer to: 'A company or organization that claims to care about breast cancer by promoting a pink ribbon product, but at the same time produces, manufactures and/or sells products containing chemicals that are linked to the disease.'

developed by Metro International Biotech. The pill, says navy commander Timothy A. Hawkins – a spokesperson for the Special Operations Command, whose mission is to advance US policies and objectives worldwide – 'is about enhancing the mission readiness of our forces by improving performance characteristics that typically decline with age.'[23] Death defiance can have imperialist ends.

It is often claimed that people – especially those living in Western cultures – are simply in denial about death. The founder of psychoanalysis Sigmund Freud wrote in 1918:

> Our attitude [towards death] had not been a sincere one. To listen to us we were, of course, prepared to maintain that death is the necessary termination of life ... In practice we were accustomed to act as if matters were quite different. We have shown an unmistakable tendency to put death aside, to eliminate it from life. We attempted to hush it up, in fact, we have the proverb: to think of something as of death. Of course we meant our own death ... in the unconscious every one of us is convinced of his immortality.[24]

It might not be, however, that we are inherently unable to reckon with death, but that we live in a culture that ushers us into ignorance or convenient amnesia. Consumerism, for example, can be understood as a form of bargaining with death; online shopping surged during the pandemic.[25] The 'post-purchase dissonance'* that consumer psychologists describe, then, might be understood as the realisation that the Thing will not save us – though realising this is unlikely to stop people trying again. The desiring itself is a kind of youth.

---

* Whereby someone feels deflated after purchasing something they had been wanting.

And when death does befall us? At least we know the bodies of our phones will outlive our own.

Our 'digital legacy' will outlast us, too. Indeed, tech companies now sell post-mortem services, arranging pre-scheduled posts to go out on deceased people's social media platforms. The posts might let 'friends' or 'followers' know you're dead, or send them birthday wishes from beyond the grave. James Norris, the founder of the platform DeadSocial,* told CNN in 2013 that the service allows users to 'literally extend the personality you had while alive in death', adding: 'We're using tech to soften the impact that death has and dehumanise it. It allows us to think about death in a more logical way and detach ourselves from it.'[26]

Long before tech services were announcing people's retirement from life on LinkedIn, however, the funeral industry was packaging death, promising to make it more bearable for a price. America's largest funeral corporation, notes the mortician and author Caitlin Doughty, has even trademarked the word 'dignity', arguing: 'What dignity translates to, more often than not, is silence, a forced poise, a rigid formality.'[27]

In 1963, the journalist Jessica Mitford – the sole communist in her aristocratic family – published a ground-breaking investigation into the funeral industry entitled *The American Way of Death*.[28] Though its context was the (white) American culture around death, its findings remain relevant to the industry's workings in many parts of the Global North, including the UK. Mitford exposed how funeral businesses harnessed the disorientating nature of grief in order to market and upsell expensive and unnecessary products and services to the bereaved. For example, she found that funeral directors usually claimed that embalming – a chemical treatment that delays the body's decomposition by replacing blood with preservatives

---

* Now called 'MyWishes'.

– was a legal requirement, when it was in fact a requirement fabricated by the industry. In profiteering from grief, argued Mitford, the funeral industry had played 'a huge, macabre, and expensive practical joke on the American public'.

The funeral industry mediates our relationship with death, via profit, arguably distancing grievers from the corporeal reality of death by obscuring decay. Of one funeral Mitford attended for her research, she writes:

> [The funeral director] has relieved the family of every detail, he has revamped the corpse to look like a living doll, he has arranged for it to nap for a few days in a slumber room, he has put on a well-oiled performance in which the concept of *death* played no part whatsoever ... He and his team have given their all to score an upset victory over death.[29]

The process of embalming itself could be understood as a battle against death fought at the expense of the living. The standard embalming fluid, formaldehyde, is a known human carcinogen – placing mortician workers at an increased risk of cancer as they delay the decomposition of the already dead.

How we bid farewell to loved ones matters; as well as celebrating their having lived, it helps us process our loss. Yet funerals, the standard 'next step' for bereavement, often take a prescriptive approach to grief – and bankrupt the grieving. Many people in the UK today face 'funeral poverty' – when the cost of a funeral (£4,000 on average), outstrips what they can afford. A 2020 report by the Competition and Markets Authority raised 'serious concerns' about the funeral industry in relation to its lack of transparency on pricing and the potential exploitation of customers' 'emotional vulnerability'.[30]

But whilst bereaved people's vulnerability is recognised for the purposes of profit, the unwieldiness of grief is rarely given space in our lives. 'Respectable' grief is private, short-lived and contained within a small circle of people. There is no statutory bereavement leave in the UK, meaning it is up to your boss whether you are permitted to take time off work to mourn – usually a few paid days at most. As with taking time off work to care for the dying, it is usually only acceptable 'professionally' to ask for leave if the deceased was a close biological relative or partner. And when we get 'back to work' we are expected to leave death at home; grieving is antithetical to productivity. Excessive mourners, argues the writer Julia Cooper, are punished: 'a socially enforced strategy of our neo-liberal era'.[31]

Grief is not supposed to be expressed in public – except for when it must be. Whilst grieving our loved ones is not supposed to interfere significantly with our productivity, rit-ualised mourning for the rich and powerful is traditionally an obligation of good citizenship. Some people are mourned publicly, with state-sanctioned fanfare – especially the royal family, benefactor and profiteer of slavery and empire. The death of Queen Elizabeth II's husband, Prince Philip, well-known to enjoy bigotry, initiated 'Operation Forth Bridge', which detailed the protocols for an eight-day period of national mourning. Flags were lowered to half-mast, children's television was suspended, news presenters wore black and radio stations played sombre music.

When his wife, 96-year-old Queen Elizabeth II, died on 8 September 2022, 'Operation London Bridge' similarly set out the minutiae of mourning – all games were banned in Royal Parks, and the day of her state funeral, costing millions, was a national holiday, for which thousands of hospital appointments were cancelled. Public space was saturated with her image and condolences – lest the people forget the royal death – and public petitions to the government were paused. The

queue of people waiting to see the monarch lying in state
stretched up to ten miles. A BBC news announcement of the
Queen's ill-health declared an important statement by the
prime minister regarding the cost-of-living crisis – which is
leaving millions struggling to survive – 'of course insignifi-
cant now' due to the 'gravity of the situation we seem to be
experiencing with Her Majesty'.[32] Later, a Sky News presenter was forced to apologise after mistakenly describing the
10 September thousands-strong protest for Chris Kaba – an
unarmed 24-year-old Black man killed by police days before
the Queen's death – as people mourning the Queen, discuss-
ing 'their memories of [her], their good wishes for the new
King'.[33] During the period of national mourning, anti-monar-
chy protestors were arrested.

In 2021, unusually, an 'ordinary' person's death also compelled national mourning. When Captain Sir John Moore died
aged 100 during the pandemic, Prime Minister Boris Johnson
urged members of the public to clap together at a particular
time in his honour. Captain Tom was a British Army veteran
who became a public figure after raising millions for the NHS
by doing sponsored laps around his garden. Whilst presid-
ing over the systematic decimation of the NHS and one of
the highest Covid-19 excess death rates in Europe, Johnson
paid tribute in Parliament to Captain Tom's efforts, saying
he 'dedicated his life to serving his country and others' and
to 'defending our nation'.[34] To the government, Captain
Tom's life was exemplary of British patriotism, and therefore
mourning it was a matter of national pride.

Most deaths do not inspire state mourning – especially not
those caused by systemic violence. When asked whether he
would 'take the knee' in honour of Black lives lost to racism,
Johnson – having called for a national clapping ritual for
Captain Tom – said he didn't 'believe in gestures'.[35] At times
of collective grief for those killed by the state, police are not

present to enforce mourning – as they are at royal funerals for instance – but to quash it. When feminists held a peaceful vigil to mourn Sarah Everard and to protest gendered violence, cops from the same force as her murderer attacked and arrested grievers, six of whom faced prosecution.

Demanding deaths

Our relationships to ageing and death are inflected by the logic of capitalism. The ways we get older, experience the end of our own and others' lives, and grieve, are culturally specific. Different peoples, in different places, at different times, have and have had vastly different feelings, beliefs and practices around death.

Not all death practices attempt denial. In *From Here to Eternity*, Doughty considers how a dominant culture of death denial in the West does a disservice to the deceased and the living, and explores different cultures of mortality. Whilst insisting there is no 'right' or 'better' way to grieve, she considers death practices that display more of a 'soft, porous border with death' than do normative Western rituals today, suggesting they might offer clues as to how to build more attuned relationships to death – and therefore to ourselves, each other and the world.[36]

Open-air cremation pyres are central to many death rituals past and present. In the UK, they have been illegal since a 1930 revision to the 1902 Cremation Act, prohibiting the fulfilment of Hindu and Sikh death rites in particular. To some believers, the prohibition of this ritual amounts to the prohibition of reincarnation. Since 2006, the founder of the Anglo Asian Friendship Society, Davender Ghai, a British Hindu who migrated to Britain from Kenya in the 1950s, has been campaigning for open-air cremations to be made possible in the UK – as a spiritual tradition as well as an alternative, low-cost option for everyone. In 2010, he won a legal battle in the court of appeal for the right to be cremated on an open-air pyre, in line with his religious beliefs. Opposing him in court was Jonathan Swift, representing the Ministry of Justice, who argued that the sacred death ritual defied 'decorum and decency'.[37]

To create better conditions for growing older, dying and grieving, we need to pay attention to the ways in which dominant ideologies and the state intensify suffering and hamper our relationships to death. In fighting for a more liveable society, we are also fighting for better deaths. Our movements for a world marked by care, safety and freedom – for housing, for healthcare, for anti-racism, for trans liberation, for climate – are part of building a world in which ageing, death and grieving well might be reclaimed as a birthright, to be experienced on our own terms, rather than a terrain of struggle. Reclaimed grief, in turn, could feed into radical movements. As the artist, educator and embodiment researcher Camille Sapara Barton writes in *The Global Environments Network Grief Toolkit*:

I imagine regular grief rituals being incorporated into movements for social change, as well as other networks as a practice of care and interdependence. Everyone will be encouraged to attend monthly grief rituals as an entry point for organising work. Communal weeping and emotional release will become normalised, held with the knowledge that this allows us to compost our feelings and make space for more presence to show up, be flexible in our thinking and operate in ways that feel aligned with our values. These grief spaces will enable us to make generative connections between our own lives, our ancestors and the stories of the lands we inhabit or are ancestrally connected with.[38]

Recognising how racism has shaped dominant ideologies and practices around death today is an essential part of creating the conditions for better deaths. The Collective for Radical Death Studies (CRDS) – 'a collective of Scholars, Funeral Directors, Death Work Practitioners, Activists, and Students of Death Studies who view death work as synonymous with anti-racism work, synonymous with actively dismantling oppression, and as a way to validate cultural and social life among marginalized groups'[39] – is working to decolonise death studies in theory and in practice. The collective aims to create change in the field by decentring whiteness, centring deathways of racialised groups and radicalising death practices, whilst underscoring the ways in which systemic oppression determines the life and death chances of marginalised groups. The group's goals are:

1. To create a Radical Death Canon that can be adapted as a tool by death educators, death scholars, death practitioners, and all those interested in understanding death, dying, and the rituals of care provided from a decolonized perspective.
2. To increase diversity in death scholarship and conversations – beyond class analysis.
3. Working to analyze how death, mourning, burial, and death investigations have changed over time along the lines of race, class, gender, ability/disability, sexuality.
4. To serve as a resource for a discerned understanding of the end-of-life experience and rituals around death for marginalized people and their communities.[40]

Liberation means remaking a world in which everyone is deserving, in which everyone's existence matters: in which everyone is grieveable. As Sara Ahmed puts it in relation to queerness: 'When queer grief is not recognized, because queer relationships are not recognized, then you become "nonrelatives", you become unrelated, you become not.'[41] Fighting for better deaths is fighting for everyone's becoming.

Care is what 'becomes' us. Currently, the care crisis is exacerbating suffering for both the cared for and carers in institutionalised and domestic settings. The care system as we know it urgently needs resourcing that reflects its value to people's quality of life and death in society as it stands. But funding is not enough. As Emma Dowling argues:

> Money will not solve the care crisis if it is used to prop up commodified care. Real change needs to address the failures of privatisation by regulating against wealth extraction and ending the competitive procurement practices that incentivise a race to the bottom. We must also radically reorganise how we care for ourselves and each other by rethinking access and ownership within care infrastructures.[42]

Dowling makes the case for 'care municipalism', to 'galvanise a strategy, bringing social care (back) under the control of public bodies, where it can be planned and delivered directly, and democratising public ownership models in partnership with communities'.[43] Ensuring better working conditions for carers is a central element of this, and indeed, care workers are fighting and winning: in 2020, outsourced adult social care workers in Bath fought to get their jobs brought back under the remit of the local authority alongside their union.[44] Resisting the care crisis is part of anti-capitalist struggle. As Dowling writes: 'if care cannot solve the problems of capitalism, capitalism is indeed preventing us from solving the problems of care. Ending the care crisis means transforming the conditions for caring. To do so requires fundamentally rethinking how to value care.'[45]

Care work is extremely underappreciated in our society because it is work historically, and mostly still, done by women – in large part working-class women from racialised groups. Such feminised labour is not seen as 'real' or 'important' work, and as such goes unrecognised and is under- or unpaid. Building a world in which caring for each other is central rather than peripheral to the organisation of our communities must be at the heart of the feminist movement. As we build a future in which everyone gets the care they need in older age and throughout their lives, we must refuse the care privations of the state and nuclear family and organise caring labour among us, as a collective and mutual endeavour.

As part of this work, we might reorient ourselves to ageing by seeking to build intergenerational networks of kin and comrades. 'We will all be old someday' must cease to be a resignation and instead become a rallying cry. Firstly, because it is not entirely true: not everyone who wishes to live a long life will, and too often this is because of structural oppression and systemic violence. Secondly, because insofar as it *is* true – in that many of us imagine we might be old one day, and in that all of us know, at least on some level, that we will die – it must not be a source of fear-based division but of solidarity.

Where the young and old are routinely pitted against each other by governments – as groups vying for limited resources, for example, or as groups who impede each other's lives – people of all ages might defy this logic by building intergenerational communities and networks of mutual aid. Just as this means integrating collective childcare into the infrastructure we build, it also means ensuring spaces are welcoming and accessible for everyone – including people towards the end of their lives.

The pandemic era offers inspiration. In responding to the urgency of survival, many local mutual aid groups took the idea that 'all we have is each other' seriously, understanding that it is all of our responsibilities to look after everyone. If older members of mutual aid groups were isolating more frequently and rigorously, for example, neighbours less vulnerable to Covid-19 supported them in meeting their needs. Radical collaborations with elders challenge the notion that older people are inevitably conservative. Recently, in both the anti-fracking movement and the campaign group Insulate Britain, older people have been visible and vocal on the frontlines of resisting the ecological crisis. In nurturing intergenerational communities of care and resistance, we might find, as Winant suggests, that 'new solidarities may form, new varieties of care, love, and responsibility may take shape – and, from them, power'.[46]

Solidarity forever

It is often said that among the most painful aspects of life is the fact that we face death alone. This reality, claims the psychotherapist Irvin D. Yalom, is one source of our 'existential isolation' – a profound form of loneliness stemming 'from the unbridgeable gap between the individual and other people'.[47] Finding ways to make each other feel held as we search for peace with our essential separateness, then, could be a radical act. Though we will, all of us, no matter what, exit aliveness alone, we are all in this together, and no one should have to do death unaccompanied.

According to the death-acceptance organisation The Order of the Good Death, founded by Doughty, being 'death positive' means believing 'that it is not morbid or taboo to speak openly about death' and seeing 'honest conversations about death & dying as the cornerstone of a healthy society'.[48] Indeed, as Barton writes, 'many traditional cultures, especially before colonisation, had collective grief practices and rituals for communities to process feelings of loss. For example, the

Dagara people of Burkina Faso have a monthly collective grief ritual that is taboo to miss. They believe that untended grief leads to harm and suffering in the collective.'[49]

Today's growing community of death doulas is attempting to cultivate more intimate experiences of death. Like birth doulas, death doulas seek to facilitate and nurture life's transitions – this might include providing support for the practical considerations of a 'good death', but also, just as importantly, negotiating and tending to the emotional landscape, alongside the dying and those close to them. Intentional relationships to death are also fostered in 'death cafés', public discussion groups where people are free to share their ideas and feelings about death, and grief circles, where people meet to tend to one another's experiences of loss. How can we create and maintain these spaces such that they are accessible, comfortable and safe for all? Building the capacity for loving mutual aid around life's transitions is an essential form of solidarity. If we trust that ourselves and our kin will be cared for at the end of our lives, we may feel less afraid of the isolation of death, and therefore be more attentive to what it could mean to be alive together. Being alive together might mean, for instance, a collective responsibility to build a world in which being alive is better.

There is power in grief because it is wild; it cannot and must not be contained. It stops us in our tracks and makes collusion with capitalist logic impossible: it may leave us unable to 'do' anything but exist. Indeed, we might grieve all that we have lost due to capitalism itself: as well as living beings, the lives we are unable to live. Grief can bring our awareness to what matters most, and in doing so be a source of radical intimacy and transformation. Grief, in this invocation, is not a solitary feeling.

Indeed, for many people, grief is always already collective, and death practices themselves can be a form of resistance. The

Chicano Movement in the United States in the 1970s, inspired by resistance among Mexicans and the Black Power movement, fought to reclaim Indigenous identity whilst fighting state oppressions, including police brutality and assimilation strategies. The movement's resistance included practising Day of the Dead (Día de los Muertos) celebrations and artistic traditions in public. To this day, Día de los Muertos rituals are part of anti-racist protest and mourning. In 2019, following the El Paso massacre in Texas, where a white nationalist targeting the Latinx community killed 23 people, mourners set up an altar with offerings near the site of the atrocity. In the shared mourning of lives lost to systemic violence, affective solidarity is radical action.

Living in the age of social media, during a global pandemic and ecological crisis, we arguably experience an especially heavy psychic burden of death. Death is not only an intimate thing we go through with those close to us, but something we are aware is happening at a magnitude and pace that it is difficult to truly comprehend. We must orientate ourselves to death such that we reckon with the ways it is unfairly, violently distributed. How can we face the grief of the world without sinking into desolation, and instead harness it to ignite collective power?

We could start by trying to accept life's evanescence. In recognising the temporariness of existence – our own, as well as that of all living beings – we might reorientate ourselves to life and comprehend afresh what is at stake in fighting for survival. This is reason to unite as well as to learn from each other: the significance of dying is not the same for everyone. In coming to terms with the many meanings of death, let us find ways to rebirth a world in which everyone is free to die – and live – well.

Conclusion: strong bonds for a fragile planet

Queer utopias are not fantasies, queer utopias are necessities!
Black Lodge Press

In the closing scene of the final episode of the television series *Friends*, the six protagonists stand sombrely in Monica and Chandler's empty Manhattan apartment, where they have all lived at some point, bidding it farewell. The couple have newborn twins and are moving to the suburbs. After Monica and Chandler place their keys on the counter, the others do the same – it turns out all of them still have a set.

'So I guess this is it…' says Phoebe to the forlorn group. 'Yeah, I guess so', sighs Joey. Monica and Rachel start to cry, and everyone comforts each other. The 'end of an era' scene is like a wake for friendship. I watched the *Friends* finale at 13, sobbing.

Friends, which ran from 1994 to 2004, is one of the most-watched television series of all time. Fan Steve Misiura proved his devotion by watching all 238 episodes, for 80 hours straight, during which time he experienced nausea and hallucinations. During its reign, *Friends* reflected and infused popular consciousness. No surprise, then, that the show was overwhelmingly white and frequently problematic. It was, too, an unrealistic depiction of New York life, not least with regards to housing. It seems implausible that the friends would have

160

been able to afford their rent.* As a child, though, I was not alert to the programme's problematics. I was fixated on it for reasons I did not understand. Like many fans, I was invested in the characters' lives, internalising their hopes and dreams to the extent that they distorted my own.

In 2021, the *Friends* cast, now in their fifties, came together for a bizarre and somehow painful reunion show, which became the most-watched broadcast ever on Sky One. During the almost two-hour long eulogy, emotional fans from all over the globe describe how watching *Friends* helped them through loneliness, mental health crises and grief. 'It became a reason for me to wake up every day', says Nancy from Ghana, 'because I felt I had friends around me'. At one point Malala is interviewed about her 'true addiction' to the show. For better and for worse, *Friends* resonated with a lot of people.

During the reunion, *Friends* co-creator Marta Kauffman explained why the series had to end when it did: 'If the show was about that time in your life when your friends are your family, once you have family of your own, it's no longer that time.' In this way, she concludes, the programme had 'a natural end'. *Friends* addressed the value of friendship, and in the group's relationships viewers could catch glimpses of enduring platonic intimacy, interdependent love beyond the couple form, and quasi-communal domesticity. Ultimately, however, all this was just a prelude. *Friends* lionised heteronormative happy endings: Ross and Rachel got back together, Monica and Chandler got their babies; Phoebe was married. Only 'eternal bachelor' Joey remained uncoupled – perhaps because he was getting his own spin-off show. 'It was really important to us to end everyone in a good place', reasoned co-creator David Crane.

---

* An explanation is offered in the final scene, with Chandler referring to 'rent control'.

'Just' friends

At 13, I thought I was so upset at *Friends* ending because I would miss the ritual of watching it. Looking back, I think my distress had something to do with a vague sense that, in the friends' seemingly preordained dispersal, their intimacy was being reneged and other possible futures denied. As Kauffman's remark identifies, the demotion of friendship is naturalised in capitalist social relations. Friendship is ascribed less value than romantic and sexual relationships, the onset of which often signals the beginning of the end, or at the least significant dilution, of platonic bonds.

Friendship is not necessarily thus. Intimacy is contingent. For example, from the eighteenth century to the early twentieth in Europe and the United States, 'romantic friendship' between women, among the bourgeois at least, was a well-recognised and prized kind of intimacy. Such friendships, whether or not they involved sex, entailed – according to the scholar of lesbian history Lillian Faderman – 'passionate commitment'.[1] By the early 1900s, however, such relationships had become socially maligned, framed as a harmful distraction from heterosexual marriage. An 1895 book, *Side Talks with Girls*, by Ruth Ashmore, cautions women against having 'a girl-sweetheart', which it claims would diminish the love available for 'Prince Charming when he comes to claim his bride'.[2]

The ancient world, as Alexandra Kollontai charts, 'considered friendship and "loyalty until the grave" to be civic virtues'. This changed, she argues, because:

Bourgeois society was built on the principles of individualism and competition, and has no place for friendship as a moral factor. Friendship does not help in any way, and may hinder the achievement of class aims; it is viewed as an unnecessary manifestation of 'sentimentality' and weakness. Friendship becomes an object of derision.[3]

Today, if we are not romantically or sexually involved with someone, we are 'just' friends. The established hierarchy for relationships – in favour of the romantic dyad and the nuclear family form – shrinks and demotes more various and comradely intimacies. This relational order can be insular and alienating not only for those who are 'single' – unable or undesirous to form a romantic partnership – but also for those who have done so and still find themselves longing for intimacy. Research shows that almost half the UK population experience feelings of loneliness.[4] Half of all older people consider television their primary companion.[5] People with long-term illness or disability are especially likely to feel lonely.[6]

The idea that being in a couple should fulfil all our intimate needs leads to desolation for many. The 'devaluation of our friendships creates an emptiness we may not see when we are devoting all our attention to finding someone to love romantically or giving all our attention to a chosen loved one',[7] writes bell hooks. And the cultural norm of neglecting friendships harms romantic partnerships, in turn. As hooks writes: 'Committed love relationships are far more likely to become codependent when we cut off all our ties with friends to give these bonds we consider primary our exclusive attention.'[8]

Friendship is conceived of as – and therefore often is – a shallower bond than a romantic partnership. As carla bergman and Nick Montgomery put it: 'Under neoliberalism, friendship is a banal affair of private preferences: we hang out, we share hobbies, we make small talk … Under neoliberal friendship, we don't have each other's backs, and our lives aren't tangled up together … Empire works to usher its subjects into flimsy relationships where nothing is at stake, and to infuse intimacy with violence and domination.'[9]

Though we may be lacking intimacy in the flesh, on social media we are pushed to 'add' friends – people we may scarcely know – to our 'network', and to share personal 'updates' with them. In 2014, the art campaign Wages for Facebook attempted to disrupt the appropriation of human relationships for profit by corporations like Facebook. Repurposing the Wages for Housework manifesto, the Wages for Facebook website announces:

THEY SAY IT'S FRIENDSHIP. WE SAY IT'S UNWAGED WORK. WITH EVERY LIKE, CHAT, TAG OR POKE OUR SUBJECTIVITY TURNS THEM A PROFIT. THEY CALL IT SHARING. WE CALL IT STEALING. WE'VE BEEN BOUND BY THEIR TERMS OF SERVICE FAR TOO LONG – IT'S TIME FOR OUR TERMS ... WAGES FOR FACEBOOK IS ONLY THE BEGINNING, BUT ITS MESSAGE IS CLEAR: FROM NOW ON THEY HAVE TO PAY US BECAUSE AS USERS WE DO NOT GUARANTEE ANYTHING ANY LONGER. WE WANT TO CALL WORK WHAT IS WORK SO THAT EVENTUALLY WE MIGHT REDISCOVER WHAT FRIENDSHIP IS.[10]

Whilst digitised 'friending' is cajoled by tech companies, other attempts at friendship are maligned and even criminalised. As we have seen, the state, offering rhetorical or material encouragement or coercion, approves of some relational forms: the biological family, the couple, the marriage, the nuclear family. It is ostensibly disinterested, meanwhile, in friendship, which is for the most part invisible in legal and policy frameworks. This apparent oversight is redressed, however, when the state considers friendship a threat to the prevailing social order. Gatherings of friends in public space, for example, are treated differently depending upon the class and race of those present. A group of working-class, house-less or Black people socialising on the streets or in a park are much more likely to face stigma and police harassment than a group of middle-class white people drinking prosecco on a picnic blanket.

For some people in the UK today, observes writer Luke de Noronha, 'friendship is dangerous'. For young Black men and boys in heavily policed urban areas, having friends is dangerous not because they endanger you, but because 'the police deem your friendships dangerous and can criminalise you for them'. Whilst being identified as a 'gang member' by the police does not correspond to criminality, it can block access to housing, education and employment – and, increasingly, it carries the threat of deportation. The racist 'gang' narrative is harnessed by the state to forge group culpability; young Black men are disproportionately charged under 'joint enterprise laws', meaning they become guilty by association. In May 2021, Manchester Crown Court found ten Black boys guilty of conspiracy to murder and grievous bodily harm. Though none of them killed anyone, they all now face lengthy prison sentences. The prosecution and press labelled the ten boys a 'gang', but what in fact connected them was the murder of a childhood friend. Evidence used against them included text messages expressing their grief and anger at the loss of their friend, as well as rap lyrics. The policing of 'gangs', writes de Noronha, 'constitutes the criminalisation of friendship'.[11]

The racist 'gang' narrative is used to criminalise allegiances that are not amenable to state power. De Noronha suggests that 'gangs' are so troubling for the state because 'they refuse the nation and make meaning and fellowship otherwise … because they do social reproduction wrong'.[12] Some forms of kinship threaten nation-building and capital by embracing the 'wrong' values and social forms.

Friendship in and against the state

Like all kinds of relationships, friendship is shackled by capitalism. To liberate it, argue bergman and Montgomery, we must recognise that, 'just as intimacy and closeness can be enabling, they can also be sources of coercion, manipulation, and exploitation. To insist on, seek out, or use friendship – and to pathologize its refusal – tends to reinforce these divisions and hierarchies rather than unravel them.'[13] How can friendship, instead, be an emancipatory source of connection, care and community? How can we build friendships that hold and sustain us as we collaborate for better futures?

As the writer, educator and trainer for transformative and disability justice Mia Mingus puts it:

> Any kind of systematic change we want to make will require us to work together to do it. And we have to have relationships strong enough to hold us as we go up against something as powerful as the state, the medical industrial complex, the prison system, the gender binary system, the church, immigration system, the war machine, global capitalism.[14]

To transform the world, we're going to need strong links between us. We must, as Mingus says, 'live out the simple truth that we need each other'.[15] For all the ways friendship is relegated and attacked, it might evade being pinned down and instead grow wings. At its best, friendship could be a liberatory relationship – one in which we can share and lessen the load of being alive. As bergman and Montgomery suggest, 'friendship as freedom … names a dangerous closeness that capitalism works to eradicate through violence, division, management, and incitements to see ourselves as isolated individuals or nuclear family units'.[16]

Foucault considers friendship's potential for counter-power in relation to homophobia, suggesting this hate is less about sex, and more about society's unease with the modes of 'affection, tenderness, friendship, fidelity, camaraderie, and companionship' that queerness spawns, as incongruous with established moulds for kinship. Dominant nodes of power, he argues, fear this kind of 'friendship' because it represents 'the formation of new alliances and the tying together of unforeseen lines of force'.[17]

The unwieldiness of friendship – understood as polyvalent intimacy that defies hierarchy, formalisation and state sanction – could be its power. In exploring this idea, we need not overhaul our established relationships; relationships tend to resist categorisation anyway, whatever their labels. A 'couple' apparently has sex, but many such relationships don't fit that definition; marriage is understood as a bond of profound emotional connection, which it often is not; a parent–child relationship is supposed to entail unfaltering care, but does not always. As we all know, relationships are 'complicated'.

Queer relationships are more likely to embrace ambiguity because queer people know that normative standards for 'real' relationships – like being straight – are a farce. If the nuclear family is more a site of harm and rejection than of love, different forms of kinship might be made more intentionally, allowing for more fluidity. Writer and performer Alok Vaid-Menon describes this beautifully in their poem 'Friendship is Romance':

i want a world where friendship is appreciated as a form of romance. i want a world where when people ask if we are seeing anyone we can list the names of all of our best friends and no one will bat an eyelid. i want monuments and holidays and certificates and ceremonies to commemorate friendship. i want a world that doesn't require us to be in a sexual/romantic partnership to be seen as mature (let alone complete). i want a movement that fights for all forms of relationships, not just the sexual ones. i want thousands of songs and movies and poems about the intimacy between friends. i want a world where our worth isn't linked to our desirability, our security to our monogamy, our family to our biology.[18]

Recently, the term 'queer platonic partner' has gained popularity. For some, this is an over-articulation of 'friendship'; for others, it is a cherished descriptor for relationships that go deeper than what is commonly understood by 'friendship'. Queer platonic partnerships might be loving commitments, involving entwinements that are ordinarily considered beyond the pale of 'just friends': perhaps cohabiting, sharing resources, fulfilling 'next-of-kin' roles or co-parenting.

bell hooks, who described 'queer' as 'the self that is at odds with everything around it',[19] wrote abundantly about the latent power of friendship as a flexible kind of love. Many women come to recognise, she argues, that heterosexual marriage alone leaves them hungry for connection: 'we may long for deep and abiding intimate bonds of communion in love that are not sexual. And yet we want these bonds to be honored cherished commitments, to bond us as deeply as marriage vows.'[20] This kind of friendship can be both enduring and transformative, she writes, because even if we make significant commitments to other people – to spouse or children, for example – it can 'change but need not be broken'.[21] Having 'deep and profound connections in friendship', she argues, 'strengthens all our intimate bonds'.[22]

With its outward-looking proclivities, in comparison to the typically insular couple form and nuclear family, friendship can incubate solidarity – and vice versa. The Lesbians and Gays Support the Miners (LGSM) group, formed to fundraise for the 1984–5 miners' strike, exemplifies political co-conspiration through friendship. After a bucket collection at the London Pride march, co-founders Mike Jackson and Mark Ashton convened a meeting, from which LGSM, and subsequently Lesbians Against Pit Closures (LAPC), grew, with groups forming across the UK. Amid the homophobia and economic cruelty of Thatcher's reign, LGSM and LAPC members joined hands with miners. Despite some initial suspicion and even hostility among the miners in receipt of the funds raised by lesbian and gay activists, striking workers from the Dulais Valley in Wales sent a representative, David Donovan, to London to meet with LGSM.

Together with LGSM members, Donovan went to a lesbian and gay pub for the first time in his life, to speak to patrons who had donated to the strike fund. After telling the crowd of around 200 about the miners' struggle, he said: 'I have been asked by the people of the Dulais Valley to extend the hand of friendship and solidarity to the lesbian and gay comrades and friends in London.'[23] In turn, LGSM and LAPC members were welcomed by mining communities, where they were greeted by a party at the miners' welfare hall. Recalling the evening of festivities, LGSM activist Robert Kincaid wrote that 'a riotous time was had by all', with gay and lesbian activists and people from the local mining community 'dancing and kissing each other'. LGSM and LAPC activists described the collective joy as 'one of the most moving experiences of all our lives'.[24]

Nurturing solidarity that is not only politically attuned but intimate can deepen our commitment to radical action. If our bonds are, as bergman and Montgomery describe, 'crucial to life, worth fighting for',[25] our struggles should reflect these highest of stakes. Sprawling intimate commitments unsettle the capitalist state, chipping away at its attempt to cache power by divide and rule. Caring for each other in indeterminate ways builds power from below, pushing back against oppressive forces. It makes sense that the state would look to undermine such bonds – especially when they straddle borders. 'It is no surprise', de Noronha notes, that 'there is no such thing as a "friendship visa"'.[26]

If friendship interrogates established hierarchies and forms of domination – in society and therefore between us – it won't be easy. Cultivating radical intimacy entails transformation of the self, of our relationships and of the world. And transformation towards brighter horizons happens through struggle, with each other, in the context of structural violence. We cannot do this without acknowledging that we, all of us, hold the potential for harm. As Mingus writes:

> we're going to mess up. Of that I am sure. We cannot, on the one hand have sharp analysis about how pervasive systems of oppression and violence are and then on the other hand, expect people to act like that's not the world we exist in. Of course there are times we are going to do and say oppressive things, of course we are going to hurt each other, of course we are going to be violent, collude in violence or accept violence as normal. We must roll up our sleeves and start doing the hard work of learning how to work through conflict, pain and hurt as if our lives depended on it – because they do.[27]

And, as Audre Lorde wrote, 'the master's tools will never dismantle the master's house'.[28] We cannot adopt the same authoritarian and punitive methods as the state, lest we repeat the kinds of violence we want to abolish. Turning towards each other for justice and repair – refusing carceral logic – demands our commitment to healing and growth in ourselves and in each other. This means learning to navigate trauma, shame and suffering. Failure to do so means risking our intimacies – and therefore our liberation struggles – as Mingus puts it, 'imploding from the inside'.[29] As we grow together, we might, as adrienne maree brown suggests, 'see ourselves as microcosms of the world, and work to shift oppressive patterns in our bodies, hearts, minds, speech, interactions, liberating ourselves into purpose, liberating our communities into new practices'.[30] Believing radical change is possible means believing it is possible in our beings and our relationships, too.

Strong bonds for a fragile planet

There is a piece of commissioned street art in my neighbourhood that says, 'SPEND YOUR TIME TOGETHER' in bold colourful lettering. Underneath, someone has sprayed: 'EASIER 4 SOME THAN OTHERS'. I first saw the words during a pandemic lockdown, reading them as a bleak reminder that many of us, through no fault of our own, are starved of intimacy. The ways we exist – are *made to exist* – under capitalism do not support intimacy. Indeed, they are often designed to fracture it. As the pandemic laid bare, normative ways of doing kinship leave many alienated, suffering and impoverished. And how we experience the intimate realm is shaped by our identities and material realities. A Black man experiencing emotional distress will not receive the same kinds of care as a white cis woman. A queer refugee will have a different experience of home and family to a middle-class British queer person. Many spaces for intimacy via collective joy – such as nightclubs and protests – are not welcoming or accessible to disabled people.

Left to its own devices, the world cannot hold us. The colliding global crises of capitalism – in ecological collapse and in the rising tide of fascism – threaten the fabric of communities and the lives that compose them. We must hold each other, as we remake a world that can. How can we create the conditions for abundant intimacy, for everyone? In the preceding chapters, I have explored some ideas, experiments and actions that will hopefully provide inspiration: psychiatric abolition and building collective care strategies such as crisis support plans; reconceiving 'family' in more expansive ways, that leave no one behind or overburdened; remaking 'home', away from the private and insular, towards communality; dismantling the supremacy of heteronormativity, for example through a feminist movement that demands sexual freedom and safety for all; transforming our collective relationship to death by finding new ways to come together in grief, such as in public rituals and vigils against state violence. Radical intimacy means germinating connection, care and community such that liberatory futures can unfurl.

Because the world as we know it is hostile to intimacy, we must be intentional about finding ways to rupture alienation. Here are some examples: befriending projects such as that run by Opening Doors, which matches LGBTQ+ people aged 50+ with queer friends, to combat isolation; taking up space on soulless commercialised streets with participatory creative pursuits, as does Street Scenes, a network that runs workshops like collage-making for passers-by; erupting spaces for public hedonism in defiance of the state, like when Kill The Bill protesters gathered in May 2021 for a post-march rave in London's Vauxhall Pleasure Gardens.

Intimacy holds radical potential because it is the kernel of being alive. Being conscious of the ways the world shapes, stifles and crushes this kernel, then, is crucial to its transformation. Perhaps *because* intimacy is so essential to our being, it can be difficult to imagine it being otherwise. Let us feed, and feed on, utopian horizons; let us come together in seizing our desires from the clutches of capitalism. Because we need stronger bonds – to hold each other together, and to keep the world from falling apart. Our mutual entwinement must be careful, spacious and supple, with no single knot tied too tight. In this macramé of loving design, we might find the wisdom, purpose and strength we need, to weave new worlds.

Some recommendations

Books

Sara Ahmed, *Living a Feminist Life* (Duke University Press, 2017)

Meg-John Barker, *Rewriting the Rules: An Anti Self-Help Guide to Love, Sex and Relationships* (Routledge, 2018)

adrienne maree brown, *We Will Not Cancel Us: And Other Dreams of Transformative Justice* (AK Press, 2020)

bell hooks, *All About Love: New Visions* (Harper Perennial, 2001)

Alex Iantaffi and Meg-John Barker, *Life Isn't Binary: On Being Both, Beyond, and In-Between* (Jessica Kingsley Publishers, 2019)

Alex Iantaffi and Meg-John Barker, *Hell Yeah Self-Care! A Trauma-Informed Workbook* (UBC Press, 2021)

Sophie Lewis, *Full Surrogacy Now: Feminism Against Family* (Verso, 2019)

Audre Lorde, *Sister Outsider* (Crossing Press, 1984)

Larry Mitchell, *The Faggots & Their Friends Between Revolutions* (Nightboat Books, 2020)

Nick Montgomery and carla bergman, *Joyful Militancy: Building Thriving Resistance in Toxic Times* (AK Press, 2017)

Torrey Peters, *Detransition, Baby* (Serpent's Tail, 2021)

Podcasts

Against Everyone with Conner Habib
All My Relations
Culture Sex Relationships with Justin Hancock (and the 'Meg-John and Justin' archive)
Death Panel
How to Survive the End of the World
In Touch with Ruby Rare
It's Not Just In Your Head: A Podcast about Capitalism and Mental Health
Raising Rebels
Rendering Unconscious with Dr Vanessa Sinclair
The Radical Therapist
Where Should We Begin? with Esther Perel

Acknowledgements

This book is not a personal achievement, but the culmination of many people's kindness, care and reflections. Special heartfelt thanks to the following people, who between them have supported me and helped me grow in ways that have been invaluable to the book's fruition – in the form of reading and giving feedback on chapters, having rich and loving conversations, caring for me in our communal home, and being affirming and encouraging when I've struggled with self-confidence: Cat Baker, Anna Corfa, Charlotte England, Zoe Ereni, Sally Evans, Sophe Gale, Grace Geilinger, Priyal Kanabar, Fiorella Leila, Matt Linares, Dan MacIntyre, Lise Masson, Laura Power, Emily Reynolds, Shaunna Rushton and Shiri Shalmy. Many others have supported me in myriad ways, too – I hope you know who you are; I appreciate you all so much.

This book also, of course, would not have been possible without all the insight and inspiration provided by other people's work, many of whom I have referenced. Special mention to Meg-John Barker and Justin Hancock, whose thinking has been instrumental to my own, and to Sophie Lewis, whose writing I find so galvanising (and who kindly gave me feedback during the book's inception).

Thanks also to the many friends and colleagues who have supported me with writing over the years – including those at Novara Media and Aeon, where I have published articles from which short extracts have been reworked in this book.

Thanks finally to everyone who has worked on the book alongside me, offering excellent, incisive feedback

Acknowledgements

and making it possible – including all those at Pluto Press, reviewers at proposal and draft stages, and editors Tim Clark and Ken Barlow.

Notes

Introduction

1. www.societyandspace.org/articles/safe-sick-isolated
2. Quoted in www.michigandaily.com/michigan-in-color/abolition-is
3. Susan Stryker, *Transgender History* (Seal Press, 2008), p. 51.
4. www.e-flux.com/architecture/artificial-labor/140680/promethean-labors-and-domestic-realism
5. Michèle Barrett and Mary McIntosh, *The Anti-social Family* (Verso, 1991), p. 139.
6. Third World Women's Alliance, Barbara A. Crow (ed.), *Radical Feminism: A Documentary Reader* (New York University Press, 2000), p. 463.
7. https://news.uchicago.edu/podcasts/big-brains/why-chasing-good-life-holding-us-back-lauren-berlant
8. https://cjds.uwaterloo.ca/index.php/cjds/article/download/212/362
9. www.versobooks.com/blogs/2499-love-s-labour-s-cost-the-political-economy-of-intimacy
10. www.weareplanc.org/blog/care-work-and-the-commons
11. adrienne maree brown, *Pleasure Activism: The Politics of Feeling Good* (AK Press, 2019), p. 13.
12. https://invertjournal.org.uk/posts?view=articles&post=7106265#gender-as-accumulation-strategy
13. https://webhome.cs.uvic.ca/~mserra/AttachedFiles/PersonalPolitical.pdf
14. David Graeber, *The Utopia of Rules: On Technology, Stupidity, and the Secret Joys of Bureaucracy* (Melville House, 2015), p. 89.

1 Your life in your hands

1. www.itv.com/news/2021-11-09/houston-police-chief-expressed-safety-concerns-to-travis-scott-before-concert
2. www.therapyden.com/news/becoming-an-online-therapist-joining-better-help-or-talkspace
3. www.maastrichtuniversity.nl/blog/2021/02/how-betterhelp-scandal-changed-our-perspective-influencer-responsibility
4. Mark Fisher, *Ghosts of My Life: Writings on Depression, Hauntology and Lost Futures* (Zero Books, 2014), p. 175.
5. Ibid.
6. www.mentalhealth.org.uk/sites/default/files/lifetime_impacts.pdf
7. www.theguardian.com/society/2020/sep/01/male-suicide-rate-england-wales-covid-19
8. www.ons.gov.uk/peoplepopulationandcommunity/wellbeing/datasets/coronavirusanddepressioninadultsingreatbritain
9. www.mind.org.uk/news-campaigns/news/existing-inequalities-have-made-mental-health-of-bame-groups-worse-during-pandemic-says-mind
10. www.theguardian.com/society/2020/dec/27/covid-poses-greatest-threat-to-mental-health-since-second-world-war
11. Mark Fisher, 'Good for Nothing', *The Occupied Times*, 19 March 2014.
12. Jamie Redman and Del Roy Fletcher, *Violent Bureaucracy: A Critical Analysis of the British Public Employment Service*, Critical Social Policy, March 2021.
13. https://novaramedia.com/2021/07/13/jobcentre-staff-were-taught-to-inflict-psychological-harm-on-the-unemployed
14. East London Big Flame, *Red Therapy* (Rye Express, 1978), p. 4.
15. www.theguardian.com/commentisfree/2021/jun/23/people-quitting-jobs-record-numbers-companies-take-note-treat-them-better
16. Erich Fromm, *To Have or to Be?* (Abacus, 1987), p. 146.
17. Malcolm Harris, *Kids These Days: Human Capital and the Making of Millennials* (Little, Brown, 2018).

18. Franco Berardi, *Precarious Rhapsody* (Minor Compositions, 2009), p. 36.
19. www.theguardian.com/technology/2018/jan/31/amazon-warehouse-wristband-tracking
20. Berardi, *Precarious Rhapsody*, p. 42.
21. https://twitter.com/d3l1b1d1n8r/status/152291741248360 8576
22. www.theguardian.com/environment/ng-interactive/2019/may/17/air-pollution-may-be-damaging-every-organ-and-cell-in-the-body-finds-global-review
23. www.imperial.ac.uk/grantham/publications/all-publications/the-impact-of-climate-change-on-mental-health-and-emotional-wellbeing-current-evidence-and-implications-for-policy-and-practice.php
24. https://lareviewofbooks.org/article/future-no-future-depression-left-politics-mental-health
25. William Davies, *The Happiness Industry: How the Government and Big Business Sold Us Well-Being* (Verso, 2015).
26. Audre Lorde, *The Cancer Journals* (spinsters/aunt lute, 1980), p. 74.
27. Sara Ahmed, *The Promise of Happiness* (Duke University Press, 2010), p. 2.
28. Ann Cvetkovich, *Depression: A Public Feeling* (Duke University Press, 2012), p. 1.
29. Mark Fisher, *K-Punk: The Collected and Unpublished Writings of Mark Fisher* (Repeater, 2018), p. 576.
30. Cvetkovich, *Depression*, p. 15.
31. www.theguardian.com/society/2022/apr/24/nhs-paying-2bn-pounds-a-year-to-private-hospitals-for-mental-health-patients
32. https://novaramedia.com/2020/02/17/marketising-the-mental-health-crisis-how-the-cbt-empire-builders-colonised-the-nhs
33. Silvia Federici and Nicole Cox, 'Counterplanning from the Kitchen' (1975), in *Revolution at Point Zero* (PM Press, 2012), pp. 35–6.

Notes

34. Theodor W. Adorno, 'Sociology and Psychology', *New Left Review*, Jan/Feb 1968, https://newleftreview.org/issues/i47/articles/theodor-adorno-sociology-and-psychology-part-ii

35. www.theguardian.com/society/2021/dec/13/nhs-trusts-urged-to-ditch-oxevision-system-covert-surveillance-mental-health-patients

36. www.change.org/p/huntercombe-hospital-maidenhead-to-be-shut-down

37. www.mind.org.uk/media-a/5135/mind-mhar-submission-final.pdf

38. Angela Y. Davis, *Are Prisons Obsolete?* (Publishers Group Canada, 2003), p. 66.

39. www.amnesty.org/en/documents/eur45/006/1997/en

40. www.rcpsych.ac.uk/improving-care/ccqi/quality-networks-accreditation/enabling-environments-network-ee

41. Jonathan Metzl, *The Protest Psychosis: How Schizophrenia became a Black Disease* (Beacon Press, 2009).

42. East London Big Flame, *Red Therapy*, p. 4.

43. www.philadelphia-association.com/history

44. https://tonybaldwinson.files.wordpress.com/2018/09/1973-people-not-psychiatry-pnp-manchester-booklet.pdf

45. Helen Spandler and Sarah Carr, 'A History of Lesbian Politics and the Psy Professions', *Feminism & Psychology* 31:1 (2021), pp. 119–39.

46. https://recoveryinthebin.org

47. https://theanarchistlibrary.org/library/campaign-for-psychiatric-abolition-there-is-no-abolition-without-anti-psychiatry

48. Meg-John Barker, 'Plural Selves, Queer, and Comics', *Journal of Graphic Novels and Comics* 11:4 (2020), pp. 463–74.

49. Mark Fisher, *Post-Capitalist Desire* (Repeater Books, 2021), p. 107.

50. www.radicaltherapistnetwork.com/qtibipoc-therapy-fund

51. www.lareviewofbooks.org/article/future-no-future-depression-left-politics-mental-health

52. East London Big Flame, *Red Therapy*, p. 11.

53. https://drive.google.com/file/d/12GItFoygeZhGRjzWa5Qj WlEepJuEoqjV/view

54. Torrey Peters, *Detransition, Baby* (Serpent's Tail, 2021), p. 99.

55. Ibid., p. 100.

56. Audre Lorde, *A Burst of Light* (Firebrand Books, 1988), p. 131.

57. Audre Lorde, *Sister Outsider* (Crossing Press, 1984), p. 173.

58. Huey P. Newton, *To Die for the People: The Writings of Huey P. Newton* (Random House, 1972), p. 104.

59. Ibid.

60. https://medium.com/@bareminimum/the-bare-minimum-manifesto-bfedbbc9dd71

61. https://johannahedva.com/SickWomanTheory_Hedva_2020.pdf

62. Kate Bornstein, *Hello, Cruel World: 101 Alternatives to Suicide for Teens, Freaks, and Other Outlaws* (Seven Stories Press, 2006), p. 96.

2 Us two against the world

1. www.independent.co.uk/news/uk/home-news/marriage-rate-uk-latest-figures-lowest-record-ons-a9464706.html

2. www.thetimes.co.uk/article/fewer-are-walking-down-the-aisle-and-divorces-surge

3. Susan Sontag, *Styles of Radical Will* (Farrar, Straus, & Giroux, 1969), p. 46.

4. https://yougov.co.uk/topics/relationships/articles-reports/2020/09/25/what-counts-established-relationship

5. Adrienne Rich, 'Compulsory Heterosexuality and Lesbian Existence', *Signs* 5:4 (1980), p. 659.

6. https://crimethinc.com/2000/09/11/adultery-and-other-half-revolutions

7. www.theguardian.com/lifeandstyle/2019/may/25/women-happier-without-children-or-a-spouse-happiness-expert

8. www.bitchmedia.org/article/bell-hooks-interview

9. Friedrich Engels, *Origin of the Family, Private Property and the State* (C.H. Kerr & Co., 1902).

10. www.liesjournal.net/volume1-03-againstcoupleform.html

11. ME O'Brien, 'To Abolish the Family: The Working-Class Family and Gender Liberation in Capitalist Development', *Endnotes* 5 (2020), p. 376.

12. Scott L. Morgensen, *The Spaces between Us: Queer Settler Colonialism and Indigenous Decolonization* (University of Minnesota Press, 2011), p. 23.

13. Leanne Betasamosake Simpson, *As We Have Always Done: Indigenous Freedom through Radical Resistance* (University of Minnesota Press, 2017), p. 110.

14. Lorde, *Sister Outsider*, p. 50.

15. Kim TallBear, 'Making Love and Relations: Beyond Settler Sex and Family', in Adele E. Clarke and Donna Haraway (eds.), *Making Kin Not Population* (Prickly Paradigm Press, 2018), pp. 147–8.

16. O'Brien, 'To Abolish the Family', p. 375.

17. Ibid., p. 376.

18. Christopher Chitty, *Sexual Hegemony* (Duke University Press, 2020), p. 25.

19. Alfie Bown, *Dream Lovers: The Gamification of Relationships* (Pluto, 2022), p. 11.

20. www.johnnycassell.com/workshops

21. www.youtube.com/shorts/8874U9HDA5I

22. www.theguardian.com/commentisfree/2018/may/12/sex-capitalism-incel-movement-misogyny-feminism

23. Amia Srinivasan, *The Right to Sex* (Farrar, Straus and Giroux, 2021).

24. https://assets.publishing.service.gov.uk/government/uploads/system/uploads/attachment_data/file/1019542/Relationships_Education__Relationships_and_Sex_Education__RSE__and_Health_Education.pdf

25. *Evening Standard Magazine*, 9 July 2021.

26. www.centreforsocialjustice.org.uk/wp-content/uploads/2009/07/CSJEveryFamilyMattersWEB.pdf

27. https://marriagefoundation.org.uk/help-us-champion-marriage-for-the-good-of-society-especially-our-children

28. www.camden.gov.uk/council-tenant-rights-responsibilities

29. https://researchbriefings.files.parliament.uk/documents/SN05051/SN05051.pdf

30. https://assets.publishing.service.gov.uk/government/uploads/system/uploads/attachment_data/file/228746/0167.pdf, p. 8.

31. Ibid., p. 11.

32. www.ted.com/talks/esther_perel_rethinking_infidelity_a_talk_for_anyone_who_has_ever_loved

33. https://web.archive.org/web/20220120200202/www.gov.uk/divorce

34. Jonathan Rauch quoted in Michael Warner, *The Trouble with Normal: Sex, Politics, and the Ethics of Queer Life* (Free Press, 1999), pp. 110–11.

35. www.tandfonline.com/doi/full/10.1080/1070289X.2021.1949814

36. Gayle Rubin, 'Thinking Sex: Notes for a Radical Theory of the Politics of Sexuality', in Carole Vance (ed.), *Pleasure and Danger: Exploring Female Sexuality* (Routledge and Kegan Paul, 1984).

37. Ibid., p. 279.

38. Ben Weil, 'No, Covid-19 Isn't a Chance to "End HIV"', *Novara Media*, 23 April 2021.

39. Ibid.

40. Sophie Lewis, 'My Octopus Girlfriend: On Erotophobia', *n+1*, Winter 2021.

41. Ibid.

42. Moira Weigel, *Labour of Love* (Farrar, Straus and Giroux, 2016).

43. Peters, *Detransition, Baby*, p. 19.

44. Ibid., p. 167.

45. https://twitter.com/reproutopia/status/1230270612033155073

46. www.frieze.com/article/love-islands-straight-camp

47. Simon May, *Love: A History* (Yale University Press, 2011), p. 4.

48. Lauren Berlant, *Desire/Love* (punctum books, 2012), p. 78.

49. Ibid., p. 79.

50. www.relate.org.uk/blog/2015/7/28/whats-emotional-affair

Notes

51. Sara Ahmed, *Living a Feminist Life* (Duke University Press, 2017), p. 48.

52. Ibid., p. 57.

53. Arlie Russell Hochschild, *The Managed Heart* (University of California Press, 1983).

54. Katherine Angel, *Tomorrow Sex Will Be Good Again: Women and Desire in the Age of Consent* (Verso, 2021).

55. Meg-John Barker, *Consent Checklist* (2019), at www.rewriting-the-rules.com/wp-content/uploads/2019/10/Consent-Checklist-1.pdf.

56. Rubin, 'Thinking Sex', p. 163.

57. Berlant, *Desire/Love*, p. 20.

58. www.marxists.org/archive/marx/works/download/pdf/18th-Brumaire.pdf, p. 5.

59. Natasha Lennard, *On Being Numerous: Essays on Non-fascist Life* (Verso, 2019), pp. 96–7.

60. https://eastendwomensmuseum.org/blog/miss-muffs-molly-house-in-whitechapel

61. Wilhelm Reich, *The Mass Psychology of Fascism* (Souvenir Press, 1997), p. 141.

62. Ibid., p. 344.

63. The Red Collective, *The Politics of Sexuality in Capitalism* (Red Collective, 1978), p. 78.

64. Ibid., p. 80.

65. Asa Seresin, 'On Heteropessimism', *The New Inquiry*, 9 October 2019.

66. Berlant, *Desire/Love*, pp. 22–3.

67. Rich, 'Compulsory Heterosexuality', p. 635.

68. https://theanarchistlibrary.org/library/mary-nardini-gang-toward-the-queerest-insurrection

69. Mel Y. Chen, *Animacies: Biopolitics, Racial Mattering, and Queer Affect* (Duke University Press, 2012), p. 104.

70. Chitty, *Sexual Hegemony*, p. 26.

71. Lorde, *Sister Outsider*, p. 57.

72. Ibid., pp. 58–9.

73. Meg-John Barker and Justin Hancock, *Make Your Own Relationship User Guide* (2016), p. 1, https://megjohnandjustin. com/product/make-your-own-relationship-user-guide-3.

74. https://theanarchistlibrary.org/library/andie-nordgren-the-short-instructional-manifesto-for-relationship-anarchy

75. bell hooks, 'The Beloved Community: A Conversation between bell hooks and George Brosi', *Appalachian Heritage* 40:4 (2012), p. 84.

76. yingchen and yingtong, 'an aromantic manifesto' (year unknown), p. 3, https://aromanticmanifesto.tumblr.com.

77. Ibid., p. 12.

78. Meg-John Barker and Alex Iantaffi, *Life Isn't Binary: On Being Both, Beyond and In-between* (Jessica Kingsley Publishers, 2019), p. 85.

79. TallBear, 'Making Love and Relations', p. 163.

80. Ibid., p. 157.

81. Ibid., p. 163.

82. www.nytimes.com/1972/04/26/archives/jury-hears-3-davis-letters-document-held-key-to-prosecution-is.html

83. www.marxists.org/archive/kollonta/1923/winged-eros.htm

84. O'Brien, 'To Abolish the Family', p. 390.

85. Fromm, *To Have or to Be?*, p. 114.

86. Ibid., p. 116.

87. Lennard, *On Being Numerous*, p. 90.

88. TallBear, 'Making Love and Relations', p. 152.

89. https://chicagoreader.com/news-politics/queer-to-the-left-came-to-raise-hell

90. Kevin A. Patterson, *Love's Not Color Blind: Race and Representation in Polyamorous and Other Alternative Communities* (Thorntree Press, 2018), p. 101.

91. Silvia Federici, *Wages against Housework* (Power of Women Collective and the Falling Wall Press, 1975), p. 6.

3 They're all you've got

1. https://people.com/music/britney-spears-dad-jamie-spears-lawyer-she-can-ask-end-conservatorship-any-time

Notes

2. https://variety.com/2021/music/news/britney-spears-full-statement-conservatorship-1235003940

3. www.nytimes.com/2021/06/22/arts/music/britney-spears-conservatorship.html

4. www.bbc.co.uk/news/world-us-canada-57839526

5. www.nytimes.com/2021/06/22/arts/music/britney-spears-conservatorship.html

6. Ibid.

7. Sophie Lewis, *Full Surrogacy Now* (Verso, 2019), p. 116.

8. www.marxists.org/archive/marx/works/1848/communist-manifesto/ch01.htm

9. David Cooper, *The Death of the Family* (Vintage Books, 1971), p. 15.

10. O'Brien, 'To Abolish the Family', p. 377.

11. TallBear, 'Making Love and Relations', p. 150.

12. https://inews.co.uk/culture/books/jacqueline-wilson-ive-tried-failed-write-happy-middle-class-families-105770

13. www.ons.gov.uk/peoplepopulationandcommunity/crimeandjustice/articles/homicideinenglandandwales/yearendingmarch2020#the-relationship-between-victims-and-suspects

14. Shulamith Firestone, *The Dialectic of Sex* (Morrow, 1970), p. 199.

15. www.independent.co.uk/news/uk/politics/boris-johnson-carrie-symonds-police-called-first-interview-bbc-brexit-a8973191.html

16. Fisher, *Post-Capitalist Desire*, p. 104.

17. Ibid., p. 101.

18. Ibid., p. 102.

19. www.opendemocracy.net/en/5050/global-anti-abortion-lgbt-rights

20. www.margaretthatcher.org/document/106689

21. www.theguardian.com/uk/2011/aug/15/david-cameron-broken-britain-policing

22. www.mirror.co.uk/tv/tv-news/anne-robinson-jibes-single-mums-23510182

23. Melinda Cooper, *Family Values: Between Neoliberalism and the New Social Conservatism* (Zone Books, 2017), p. 105.

24. Ibid., pp. 8–9.

25. https://assets.publishing.service.gov.uk/government/uploads/system/uploads/attachment_data/file/947066/family-reunion-guidance-v5.0ext.pdf

26. www.thedigradio.com/transcripts/transcript-abolish-the-family-with-sophie-lewis

27. https://fabians.org.uk/publication/the-road-ahead

28. Ibid., p. 31.

29. Ibid., p. 20.

30. https://twitter.com/fraserstweets/status/1475590972755087364

31. https://twitter.com/lolaolufemi_/status/1232596688923242497

32. Hortense J. Spillers, 'Mama's Baby, Papa's Maybe: An American Grammar Book', *Diacritics* 17:2 (1987), pp. 74.

33. Ibid., pp. 74–5.

34. https://uca.edu/training/files/2020/09/black-Lives-Matter-Handout.pdf

35. www.patreon.com/posts/abolish-60456912

36. O'Brien, 'To Abolish the Family', p. 417.

37. Loretta J. Ross, Preface to Alexis Pauline Gumbs, China Martens and Mai'a Williams (eds.), *Revolutionary Mothering: Love on the Front Lines* (PM Press, 2016), p. xv.

38. Gumbs et al. (eds.), *Revolutionary Mothering*, p. 20.

39. Ibid., p. 22.

40. https://twitter.com/PepePierce/status/1446117561486086157

41. https://twitter.com/UR_Ninja/status/1429805044879273988

42. Lewis, *Full Surrogacy Now*, p. 167.

43. http://gutsmagazine.ca/theses-on-postpartum

44. TallBear, 'Making Love and Relations', p. 156.

45. www.societyandspace.org/articles/safe-sick-isolated

46. Armistead Maupin, *Logical Family: A Memoir* (HarperCollins, 2017).

47. https://newsocialist.org.uk/infamous-proposal

Notes

48. Adrienne Rich, *Of Woman Born: Motherhood as Experience and Institution* (New York: Norton, 1976).

49. Gumbs et al. (eds.), *Revolutionary Mothering*, p. 21.

50. Ibid., p. 26.

51. Quoted in ibid., p. 28.

52. bell hooks, *Outlaw Culture: Resisting Representations* (Routledge, 2006), p. 249.

53. https://bigflameuk.files.wordpress.com/2009/10/childrensc.pdf

54. Ibid.

55. https://fabians.org.uk/publication/the-road-ahead

56. O'Brien, 'To Abolish the Family', p. 410.

57. Ibid.

58. Lauren Berlant, *Cruel Optimism* (Duke University Press, 2011), p. 1.

59. Ibid., p. 19.

60. https://newsocialist.org.uk/infamous-proposal

61. https://theoccupiedtimes.org/?p=13482

62. Betasamosake Simpson, *As We Have Always Done*, p. 10.

63. Ibid., p. 9.

64. Nick Montgomery and carla bergman, *Joyful Militancy: Building Thriving Resistance in Toxic Times* (AK Press, 2017), p. 101.

65. Barrett and McIntosh, *The Anti-social Family*, p. 147.

66. Kai Cheng Thom, *I Hope We Choose Love: A Trans Girl's Notes from the End of the World* (Arsenal Pulp Press, 2019), p. 115.

67. Ibid., p. 113.

68. Ibid., p. 119.

69. Lewis, *Full Surrogacy Now*, p. 78.

70. Montgomery and bergman, *Joyful Militancy*, p. 101.

71. TallBear, 'Making Love and Relations'.

72. Barker and Iantaffi, *Life Isn't Binary*, p. 85.

73. Barrett and McIntosh, *The Anti-social Family*, p. 139.

74. Ibid., p. 141.

4 A ladder is not a resting place

1. https://criticalspatialpractice.co.uk/asset-arrest-2016

2. www.architectsjournal.co.uk/news/som-designed-block-acted-like-broken-chimney-fire-report-finds

3. www.insidehousing.co.uk/news/news/developer-sent-cease-and-desist-letter-by-trustpilot-over-five-star-reviews

4. www.londoncityisland.com

5. www.trustforlondon.org.uk/data/boroughs/newham-poverty-and-inequality-indicators

6. www.newhamrecorder.co.uk/news/newham-rent-wage-ons-figures-3248152

7. Kristian Niemietz, *Left Turn Ahead? Surveying Attitudes of Young People Towards Capitalism and Socialism* (Institute for Economic Affairs, 2021).

8. https://commonslibrary.parliament.uk/research-briefings/sn03668

9. Fisher, *Post-Capitalist Desire*, p. 108.

10. www.stonewall.org.uk/system/files/lgbt_in_britain_-_trans_report_final.pdf

11. www.theguardian.com/uk-news/2021/jan/28/no-10-pulls-sexist-covid-ad-showing-all-chores-done-by-women

12. Federici, *Wages against Housework*, p. 2.

13. Ibid., p. 3.

14. www.thenation.com/article/society/family-covid-care-marriage

15. Out of the Woods collective, *Hope against Hope: Writings on Ecological Crisis* (Common Notions, 2020), p. 57.

16. Angela Mitropoulos, *Contract and Contagion: From Biopolitics to Oikonomia* (Autonomedia, 2013), p. 28.

17. www.theguardian.com/uk-news/2018/mar/05/st-mungos-homeless-charity-helped-target-rough-sleepers-to-deport

18. www.opendemocracy.net/en/opendemocracyuk/uk-gypsies-and-travellers-take-stand-against-discrimination-0

19. bell hooks, *Yearning: Race, Gender, and Cultural Politics* (South End Press, 1990), p. 387.

Notes

20. www.unhcr.org/uk/60950ed64/unhcr-observations-on-the-new-plan-for-immigration-uk

21. Out of the Woods collective, *Hope against Hope*, p. 61.

22. www.theguardian.com/commentisfree/2021/may/18/amazon-ring-largest-civilian-surveillance-network-us

23. www.statista.com/statistics/956906/burglaries-in-england-and-wales

24. www.theguardian.com/uk-news/2021/oct/14/amazon-asks-ring-owners-to-respect-privacy-after-court-rules-usage-broke-law

25. www.businessinsider.com/amazon-ring-patents-describe-cameras-recognizing-skin-texture-odor-2021-12

26. Daniel Miller et al., *The Global Smartphone: Beyond a Youth Technology* (UCL Press, 2021), p. 219.

27. www.e-flux.com/architecture/artificial-labor/140680/promethean-labors-and-domestic-realism

28. www.thenation.com/article/society/family-covid-care-marriage

29. www.opendemocracy.net/en/oureconomy/coronavirus-crisis-shows-its-time-abolish-family

30. Federici, *Wages against Housework*, p. 5.

31. Ibid., p. 3.

32. Ibid., pp. 2–3.

33. www.theguardian.com/world/2015/aug/03/europeans-who-welcome-migrants

34. Berlant, *Desire/Love*, p. 22.

35. www.artforum.com/print/199209/the-body-you-want-an-inteview-with-judith-butler-33505

36. hooks, *Yearning*, pp. 385, 384.

37. Sheila Rowbotham, *Daring to Hope: My Life in the 1970s* (Verso, 2021).

38. www.societyandspace.org/articles/safe-sick-isolated

39. Susan Fraiman, *Extreme Domesticity* (Columbia University Press, 2017), p. 5.

40. https://lgbtiqoutside.org/our-mission

41. www.instagram.com/p/CM-fhSdFbfh

42. https://freedomnews.org.uk/2021/12/07/autonomous-winter-shelter-opened-in-former-st-mungos-hostel

43. Out of the Woods collective, *Hope against Hope*, p. 59.

44. Ibid.

45. Fisher, *Post-Capitalist Desire*, p. 105.

46. Larry Mitchell, *The Faggots & Their Friends Between Revolutions* (Nightboat Books, 2020), p. 83.

47. Firestone, *The Dialectic of Sex*, p. 231.

48. Ibid., p. 324.

49. Lewis, *Full Surrogacy Now*.

5 The great equaliser

1. https://warwick.ac.uk/fac/arts/english/currentstudents/postgraduate/masters/modules/postcol_theory/mbembe_22necropolitics22.pdf

2. www.theguardian.com/environment/2021/nov/16/indigenous-climate-activists-cop26-endangers-native-communities

3. www.inquest.org.uk/deaths-in-police-custody

4. www.statista.com/statistics/296698/local-areas-with-highest-male-life-expectancy-united-kingdom-uk

5. www.randoxhealth.com

6. UN Human Rights Council, *Report of the Special Rapporteur on Extreme Poverty and Human Rights, Philip Alston* (2019), p. 1.

7. Ibid.

8. Lorde, *A Burst of Light*, p. 119.

9. Anne Boyer, *The Undying: A Meditation on Modern Illness* (Penguin, 2019), pp. 156–7.

10. www.un.org/en/global-issues/ageing

11. https://commonslibrary.parliament.uk/research-briefings/cbp-9239

12. www.alzheimers.org.uk/about-us/policy-and-influencing/what-we-think/dementia-tax

13. www.nplusonemag.com/issue-30/reviews/not-every-kid-bond-matures-2

Notes

14. www.tuc.org.uk/research-analysis/reports/new-deal-social-care-new-deal-workforce

15. Katie Roiphe, *The Violet Hour: Great Writers at the End* (Random House, 2016), p. 40.

16. https://radicaldeathstudies.com/2019/08/10/decolonizing-death-studies

17. https://ageing-better.org.uk/news/mocking-patronising-and-demonising-uks-ageist-attitudes-revealed-new-report

18. www.ageuk.org.uk/globalassets/age-uk/documents/reports-and-publications/consultation-responses-and-submissions/health--wellbeing/loneliness-and-covid-19---december-2021.pdf

19. www.dissentmagazine.org/article/grief-circling

20. Boyer, *The Undying*, p. 86.

21. Ibid., p. 315.

22. Fromm, *To Have or to Be?*, p. 126.

23. www.genengnews.com/news/u-s-special-operations-command-to-test-anti-aging-pill

24. Sigmund Freud, *Reflections on War and Death* (White Press, 2014), p. 20.

25. www.theguardian.com/business/2021/dec/31/online-shopping-pets-and-takeaways-fuel-surge-in-uk-spending-in-2021

26. https://edition.cnn.com/2013/02/22/tech/social-media/death-and-social-media

27. Caitlin Doughty, *From Here to Eternity: Traveling the World to Find the Good Death* (Weidenfeld and Nicolson, 2017), p. 102.

28. Jessica Mitford, *The American Way of Death* (Simon and Schuster, 1963).

29. Ibid., p. 77.

30. https://assets.publishing.service.gov.uk/media/5fdb557e8fa8f54d5733f5a1/Funerals_-_Final_report.pdf

31. Julia Cooper, *The Last Word: Reviving the Dying Art of Eulogy* (Coach House Books, 2017), p. xx.

32. www.huffingtonpost.co.uk/entry/clive-myrie-clarifies-comments-energy-crisis-during-queen-bbc-broadcast-backlash_uk_631b1238e4b0eac9f4d65d97

33. www.theguardian.com/media/2022/sep/11/sky-news-apologises-for-report-mistaking-chris-kaba-protest-for-royal-crowds

34. https://hansard.parliament.uk/commons/2021-02-03/debates/2177E714-0248-4F3B-BE41-6EC94D176060/Engagements

35. www.independent.co.uk/news/uk/politics/boris-johnson-take-knee-black-lives-matter-protests-a9599301.html

36. Doughty, *From Here to Eternity*, p. 75.

37. www.theguardian.com/world/2010/feb/10/hindu-cremation-pyre-appeal

38. https://globalenvironments.org/toolkits/grief-toolkit, p. 37.

39. https://radicaldeathstudies.com/about-crds

40. Ibid.

41. Ahmed, *The Promise of Happiness*, p. 109.

42. https://novaramedia.com/2020/09/29/money-alone-wont-fix-the-care-crisis-we-need-a-radical-rethink

43. Ibid.

44. https://southwest.unison.org.uk/news/2020/01/adult-social-care-services-back-council-control-bath

45. Emma Dowling, *The Care Crisis: What Caused It and How Can We End It?* (Verso, 2021), p. 353.

46. www.nplusonemag.com/issue-30/reviews/not-every-kid-bond-matures-2

47. Irvin D. Yalom, *Staring at the Sun: Overcoming the Terror of Death* (Jossey-Bass, 2008), p. 121.

48. www.orderofthegooddeath.com/death-positive-movement

49. https://globalenvironments.org/toolkits/grief-toolkit, p. 4.

Conclusion: strong bonds for a fragile planet

1. Lillian Faderman, *Surpassing the Love of Men: Romantic Friendship and Love between Women, from the Renaissance to the Present* (Morrow, 1981), p. 16.

2. Lillian Faderman, *Odd Girls and Twilight Lovers: A History of Lesbian Life in Twentieth-Century America* (Columbia University Press, 1991), p. 50.

3. www.marxists.org/archive/kollonta/1923/winged-eros.htm

4. www.campaigntoendloneliness.org/the-facts-on-loneliness

5. www.ageuk.org.uk/globalassets/age-uk/documents/reports-and-publications/reports-and-briefings/health--wellbeing/rb_june15_lonelines_in_later_life_evidence_review.pdf

6. www.campaigntoendloneliness.org/the-facts-on-loneliness

7. bell hooks, *All About Love: A New Vision* (Harper Perennial, 2001), p. 135.

8. Ibid.

9. Montgomery and bergman, *Joyful Militancy*, p. 93.

10. http://wagesforfacebook.com

11. www.historyworkshop.org.uk/gangs-policing-deportation-and-the-criminalisation-of-friendship

12. Ibid.

13. Montgomery and bergman, *Joyful Militancy*, pp. 124.

14. https://leavingevidence.wordpress.com/2012/08/03/on-collaboration-starting-with-each-other

15. Ibid.

16. Montgomery and bergman, *Joyful Militancy*, p. 82.

17. Michel Foucault, *Ethics: Subjectivity and Truth* (New Press, 1997), p. 136.

18. www.alokvmenon.com/blog/2017/2/15/friendship-is-romance. See also Alok Vaid-Menon, *Femme in Public* (8-Ball Community, 2017).

19. www.youtube.com/watch?v=rJkohNROvzs

20. bell hooks, *Communion: The Female Search for Love* (Morrow, 2002), p. 208.

21. Ibid.

22. hooks, *All About Love*, p. 136.

23. http://lgsm.org/our-history/228-lesbians-and-gays-support-the-miners

24. Polly Vittorini, Nicola Field and Caron Methol, 'Lesbians against Pit Closures', in Vicky Seddon (ed.), *The Cutting Edge: Women and the Pit Strike* (Lawrence & Wishart, 1986), p. 144.

25. Montgomery and bergman, *Joyful Militancy*, p. 96.
26. www.historyworkshop.org.uk/gangs-policing-deportation-and-the-criminalisation-of-friendship
27. https://leavingevidence.wordpress.com/2012/08/03/on-collaboration-starting-with-each-other
28. Audre Lorde, *The Master's Tools Will Never Dismantle the Master's House* (Penguin Classics, 2018), p. 19.
29. https://leavingevidence.wordpress.com/2012/08/03/on-collaboration-starting-with-each-other
30. http://adriennemareebrown.net/2013/02/05/coevolution-through-friendship

Thanks to our Patreon subscriber:

Ciaran Kane

Who has shown generosity and
comradeship in support of our publishing.

Check out the other perks you get by subscribing
to our Patreon – visit patreon.com/plutopress.

Subscriptions start from £3 a month.